7 PEOPLE WHO CAN DESTROY Your BUSINESS Or CAREER

Identify Them Early. Protect Your Growth.

7 PEOPLE WHO CAN DESTROY Your BUSINESS Or CAREER

Identify Them Early. Protect Your Growth.

Amita Vikram Pratap

Available on amazonkindle

Worldwide Published by

Pendown Press

PREMIUM BUSINESS PUBLISHER

PENDOWN PRESS LLP

An ISO 9001 & ISO 14001 Certified Co.,

Regd. Office: 3767A, Kanhaiya Nagar,

Tri Nagar, Delhi-110035

Ph.: 8130886000, 9650072927

E-mail: info@pendownpress.com

Branch Office: 1A/2A, 20, Hari Sadan, Ansari Road,

Daryaganj, New Delhi-110002

Ph.: 011-45794768

Website: PendownPress.com

Edition: 2026

Price: ₹ 299

ISBN: 978-93-7217-234-8

Layout and Cover Designed by Pendown Graphics Team

DISCLAIMER

This book is a work of narrative nonfiction inspired by the author's observations and experiences in professional and personal environments. Certain names, characters, companies, organizations, locations, and identifying details have been altered or fictionalized to protect the privacy of individuals.

Any resemblance to actual persons, living or dead, businesses, organizations, or events is purely coincidental and unintended.

The personality types, scenarios, and situations described in this book are presented as illustrative interpretations of human behaviour and are not intended to portray or identify any specific individual or entity.

Any references to brand names, trademarks, or companies are used solely for narrative or illustrative purposes and do not imply endorsement, association, or factual representation. Such references have no bearing on the themes, analysis, or conclusions presented in this book.

The views and interpretations expressed in this work are solely those of the author and are intended for educational, informational, and reflective purposes.

DEDICATION

To Naresh and Sunita, my Papa and Mummy, who taught me integrity before ambition.

To Maheya, my beautiful daughter, so that one day you know your mother chose courage over silence.

And to Vikram, my husband, who walked beside me through the storms that shaped this story.

TABLE OF CONTENTS

ABOUT THE AUTHOR

Amita Vikram Pratap is an Authority Builder and Brand Romance Expert, dedicated to helping people and businesses build powerful brands that command trust, attention, and influence.

With over two decades of experience in branding, communication, and narrative strategy, she has worked with global corporations, SMEs, and visionary founders to transform products, services, and leaders into recognized authorities in their fields.

Through her signature frameworks, MAV (Make Authority Visible) and the MAVERICK Framework for unique storytelling, Amita blends psychology, emotion, and strategy to help brands uncover their essence, shape perception, and convert attention into economic value.

As an Authority Builder, Amita believes that a powerful brand should enter the room before the person does, through reputation, narrative, and credibility.

As a Brand Romance Expert, she believes the strongest brands are not merely seen or heard, they are loved, trusted, and remembered.

She is the founder of MAV Brand Stories, a strategic storytelling consultancy based in the UAE, built on a simple belief: every brand has a heartbeat, waiting for the right story to make it heard.

But Amita's work is not shaped only by boardrooms and brand strategy. Her journey has also been deeply personal, from experiencing loss to rediscovering strength, and from betrayal to breakthrough. These lived experiences inspired her to write "Seven People Who Can Destroy Your Business or Career," a book born not from theory, but from the real and often difficult realities of navigating power, trust, and human behaviour in business and life.

Beyond her professional achievements, Amita holds her identities close to her heart: first, a daughter, then a wife, and a mother.

"Businesses rarely collapse because of markets; they collapse because of people."

Connect with Amita Vikram Pratap

LinkedIn: linkedin.com/in/amitavikrampratap

Email: amita@mavbrandstories.com

Website: www.mavbrandstories.com

AUTHOR'S NOTE

There comes a hush when wars move from bustling streets to the quiet corridors of the soul –

where trust duels with betrayal, and instinct dances with illusion in the silent dark.

My goal with "*7 People Who Can Destroy Your Business or Career*" is to reveal the human archetypes (deep patterns) that impact a business or employment life. We aim to caution instead of instilling fear. Every story in this book feels personal, even if not all are my own. Sometimes I was directly involved, sometimes merely a witness, and often, just a listener.

I began drafting this book driven by feelings of revenge, anger, and frustration. I intended to give voice to my pain, reveal the deceptions and masks people use, and caution others about the cruelty the world shows to innocent hearts. Yet as I progressed, I noticed a repeating pattern, one that transcends offices, industries, and relationships.

Throughout this journey, I understood that protecting one's career and business goes far beyond contracts or clauses. It means safeguarding your energy, your time, and your truth.

The people who inflict the deepest wounds rarely come under the spotlight themselves; instead, they shine as opportunities, partners, or friends. Their presence is a reminder that business involves not just strategy, but also psychology. Every manipulation you overcome earns you a PhD in human behaviour, and every betrayal you unravel sets a new boundary.

With each chapter, I found myself revisiting those moments, not as a victim, but as an observer. The book became something deeper: a journey of self-reflection and a personal confrontation between my truth and the world's.

- Some chapters will help you recognise others, while some will invite self-awareness.
- For me, it is the closure of a chapter in my soul; for you, I hope, it becomes armour for your professional journey.

As I juggled between managing responsibilities, *Swarangi Songire (Creative Freelancer)* supported with chapter completion. Heartfelt acknowledgement and appreciation to her and also to her family, whose faith has given her the strength to work diligently.

I express my gratitude to everyone who has, knowingly or unknowingly, contributed to my journey and made this book possible. I owe every word in this book to the people who tested my strength and those who helped me find it again!

PROLOGUE
THE RISE OF THE FALL

Behind every crisis, there is a story of character, of behaviour, and of a human.

Over four decades of living, two of them immersed in working with people, I have witnessed the quiet architecture of failure. The primary lesson was the most personal: my father's business empire, once thriving, slowly came apart at the seams. Its collapse involved everyone, partners, colleagues, clients, and family, quietly marking the start of my real education. Since then, I have learned and unlearned many lessons in work ethics, loyalty, and leadership. And one truth has stayed constant:

No empire is lost to rivals; it is destroyed when our own people undermine trust.

- One overlooked employee.
- One compromise for a relative.
- One person we trust implicitly.

The people you hire, confide in, or give second chances can become your greatest assets or your greatest liabilities.

- Some drain your energy.
- Others disrupt your teams.
- A few quietly undermine your foundation until, one day, you realise that the downfall is incremental, almost invisible, until it is impossible to ignore.

THE PROMISE

By the end of this book, you will not just see them, but you will see yourself. The versions that yielded, the instincts that stayed silent, the strength that has been waiting to return. You will learn to protect your purpose without losing your softness. To read the signs without building walls. To find meaning in what fell apart — a lesson in every betrayal, a reflection in every manipulation, a quiet beginning in every end.

Because in business & beyond, awareness is wealth before money; boundaries are peace before success.

THE SEVEN ARCHETYPES

Seven represents more than a simple figure; it is a recurring pattern woven throughout the universe:

- Seven colours form the rainbow
- Seven notes define a musical scale
- Seven chakras align the body.
- Seven days of the week
- And the mind naturally groups information in sevens.

This number marks the intersection of order and mystery; the edge of human understanding.

This book is about those seven archetypes - the known yet unknown saboteurs who come in many forms (in boardrooms) and minds (in behaviour) follow that same rhythm. Each one is an energy - a behavioural virus shaping thought, culture, and consequence. Together, they form the full spectrum of the human psyche.

This book is a meet & greet with:

- The **SNAKE**, the charmer and deceiver
- The **TERMITE**, who weathers you from within
- The **CUCKOO**, orchestrating things from the shadows
- The **FLY**, thriving amidst chaos
- The **DONKEY**, steadfastly resisting every change you attempt
- The **HYENA** and the **OCTOPUS**, who mask their true intentions behind laughter and luxury while quietly controlling and consuming those around them.

This book is not a management manual. Instead, it presents a thesis devoted to awareness, acceptance, and acknowledgement. It is about perceiving people from a different perspective and applying that same viewpoint to yourself. To read others, you must first learn to read yourself.

Each archetype will inspire you to ask yourself difficult questions:

- Why did I attract this kind of person?
- What did I ignore in my gut?
- What lesson was I meant to learn before it became a loss?

This is where stories of transformation evolve from being simple reactions to thoughtful reflections.

CHAPTER 1

THE FLY
FAST TO LEECH OFF YOU

A Season of Betrayal

Not even a season had passed. Dubai's heat still clung to the glass of every skyscraper when the betrayal surfaced.

It was a late evening and a long drive through Jumeriah. A billboard towered above the traffic with a French Limestone palette and Arabian Dusk accents.

The tagline: ***"Designs worth stealing".*** The very line pulled from Slide 17 of *Ad'luxe's* pitch deck.

The influencer posed in the frame - the same woman *Ira, CCO,* had painstakingly shortlisted.

Even the store mock-up was identical: arches softened with desert tones, the floor tiles matching the cobblestones *Brutus* had once praised.

Every detail was theirs. Every credit chiselled out of Ad'Luxe's team.

Étagère Affair*, a French Furniture Brand,* had arrived in Dubai like royalty with empty suitcases, promising grand expansions, influencer soirées, and bespoke product launches. There were handshakes, promises of vendor meetings, and nods about commercials.

The Ad'luxe team had burned through nights, Teams messages glowing with urgency and trust. Their pitch carried the weight of endless caffeine and quiet ambition. Ira had carried Brutus' lurky words like gospel: *"You see the nuances here, the way we see the cobblestones of our streets."*

As the clock ticked, the void emerged with the slow drip of unanswered emails and messages. What followed was emotional chaos with: *Confusion:* ***"Did we miss something?", Shame: "How do I face my team now?", and Overthinking: "Maybe it was too much, too soon."***

On Jumeirah's stretch, Ira sat stalled at a red light, the light washing her face in a rage, tinged with shame, and betrayal she could not hide.

Her and her team's vision shining in coloured and shiny stones on the billboard felt like a silent mockery of their efforts.

Ira's mind spat the only words that fit: *Et tu, Brute?*

Brutus' team left no wounds, just traces, as a FLY does.

The Anatomy of a Buzz

FLY-type personalities are those who appear to be full of energy, curiosity, and praise and will hover endlessly in your space, not to help, support, or develop, but to drain emotional energy, escalate their suffering, and distract you with incessant buzzing about their problems.

- They may seem harmless, even pitiable, but make no mistake: flies thrive on attention and disorder.
- Their helplessness is not genuine; it is a tactic.
- They are not always malicious; their behaviour is patterned as opportunistic, transactional, and hollow beneath the surface, and that is what makes them dangerous.

The Corporate Jungle Where They Thrive

In the corporate ecosystem, the FLY breathes and thrives in all nooks and corners. Within organisations, they hover around high-performing teams, mimicking inputs, echoing meetings, and slowly climbing upward on the back of other people's momentum.

These individuals will seek the mid-level thrones where visibility is high, but accountability remains low, the ideal altitude to hover, mimic, and manoeuvre without real risk.

In strategy meetings, they repeat ideas before the originator finishes and are quick to claim credit or deflect blame. Masters at blending in, camouflaging as collaborators, and they rise by attaching to others' success, making superficial impressions that substitute for genuine contributions. This "copy-paste" culture stifles innovation, which is why such people rarely become CEOs, as those roles require true vision.

Gail, The F-Leader!

Gail was never supposed to lead.

Once upon a boardroom shift of Doha's largest shipping conglomerates, Gail, a Commercial Director, was handed the CEO crown for the regional office. He was decent with paperwork, client flattery, and known for echoing what bosses wanted to hear.

Now, power had exposed him.

From day one, it was clear: He built nothing, only feasted on inflated praise and silenced dissent.

As months blurred into years, the true builders left.

A chill took the halls. Raises faded, workloads swelled, and complaints dissolved in silence.

Still, Gail broadcast positivity, quoting numbers and optimism at every town hall while the company bled talent and trust behind the scenes.

And still… the flyways never traced their flight home.

Ownership watched, distant and hopeful, for three years, long enough for mediocrity to root deeply.

By the time the FLY was swatted from the CEO's chair, the real damage was done: the best talent was gone, and the company's reputation as an employer had suffered.

It was a planned admiration, not theft.

The FLY left trust in tatters.

Gia Got Houdini-Ed

For Gia, the call felt like destiny.

Gia, a strategist hungry for her next leap, had found a role at Pitch Please, a rising agency that seemed to "get" her even before she spoke.

The first call went well, and she was sent a "quick test" to prove how much out-of-the-box thinking she is capable of doing.

Gia treated it like a real pitch.

"How you do anything is how you do everything," they say, and she showed up like it was Day One.

She pulled late nights

Researched trends

Stitched insights into crisp copy

And built a concept that was both fresh and intuitive.

When she submitted it, she imagined herself working at her dream desk.

Days flew by. Calls and Emails hung unanswered. No follow-up, no acknowledgement from the agency end.

Weeks later, scrolling LinkedIn, Gia's gut ached.

There it was: her idea, polished and posted on the agency's page.

Same skeleton, different skin. No credit. Just quiet theft.

Anxiety kicked in her chest like a swarm of flies, buzzing without pause. At night, she replayed the calls. "How could they smile, promise, and then vanish with my work?

I was not just Houdini-ed but robbed. And now, I have to choose between staying small or fighting louder."

For Gia, it was not just about losing an opportunity but losing trust in the entire corporate system.

Clean Jungle, Happy Culture

Though FLY personalities might appear minor, their presence corrodes team dynamics on a broader level with minimal to no contribution, draining ideas, and fostering mistrust. Eliminating the "buzz" restores clarity and encourages genuine creativity, leading to a fair, collaborative, and innovative culture, ensuring energy is invested where it matters.

Pattern Recognition, Not Paranoia

A FLY's buzz is never harmless. It is the sound of your effort being siphoned away.

Here are the patterns that reveal when you are dealing with one:

- **Intellect Drainers:** They challenge your thinking endlessly but without direction. Every conversation demands attention yet lacks real purpose, leaving you mentally exhausted.
- **Shortcut Addicts:** Obsessed with quick wins, they trumpet big ambitions but avoid NDAs, contracts, or clear scopes. Their pattern is request-heavy, commitment-light.
- **Stakeholder Smokescreens:** There is always "one more person" to convince, or crises to justify delays like personal emergencies, made-up health excuses, or shifting priorities.
- **Creative Parasites:** Insecure to create, too proud to collaborate, they mine brilliance from eager talent. They lure with promises of "future work" but seek free consulting.
- **Theft as Curation:** Ownership is irrelevant as long as execution masks the source. They do not see stealing as wrong. For them, borrowing ideas is "smart curation."
- **Master Deflectors:** Accountability is kryptonite for them. Once confronted, they vanish. In person, they feign ignorance; online, they ghost you.

- **Emotional Escape Artists:** They thrive in ambiguity, avoiding closure, dodging decisions, staying in perpetual limbo. Out of sympathy, you over-function, draining yourself further.

Dealing With the "Drama" Without any Drama

Dealing with the FLY needs filtration, not fights.

FLY-proofing begins with being intentional about self-boundaries and time. Stating terms clearly and confidently in proposals, onboarding emails, and every conversation about work establishes the value of time and communication upfront.

Instead of diving headfirst into ideation, start with intention.

Ask the questions that reveal their purpose:

- *"Are you looking for a partner, or mere perspective?"*
- *"What is the timeline?"*
- *"When do we formalise the scope?"*

A phrase like, "*This session is complimentary; anything further is part of our paid scope,*" filters out fluff and people who do not respect you.

Treating time like currency prevents oneself from slipping into unpaid consulting under the guise of "just another iteration."

Track how much is given and let the documentation serve as an invisible shield, reassuring both the client and you of the professional approach. People will think twice if they know you are organised and assertive. For follow-ups, two attempts are enough; anything more is generosity, not pursuit.

Before sharing anything that holds weight, protect it with an NDA, a watermark, or a disclaimer tucked into the document.

These are quiet contracts with and for oneself that avoid mistrust. It is important to remember and follow that it is not your business to entertain freeloaders with a free show.

If someone often leaves you feeling uncertain, undervalued, or drained, remember they are not the missing piece in your puzzle. Do not let them chip away, even subtly. Safeguard your peace and priorities. After all, your creativity is not an *'all-you-can-eat'* buffet.

An Invoice In Limbo

Several years ago, **Betelgeuse Agency** joined forces with **Nova Studios**, an entertainment production house celebrated for launching rising talent. While Nova had lost its lustre amid swirling rumours of financial mismanagement, their relaunch aimed to restore their former glory.

With a composed tone belying the urgency in her eyes, Luna, the CEO of Nova Studios, said, "This is our make-or-break. One last push, and you will be etched into our success story." Aster, the brand manager, leaned in, smirked, her voice softening to a conspiratorial tone as she had read eager Luna's mind: "Betelgeuse is not just a partnership; you are family. This means more than business."

Betelgeuse Agency, recalling earlier collaborations, believed them and devoted itself to the campaign. Demeter, the Creative Director, often stayed late, lingering over unfinished presentations and whispering, "If they rise, we rise. If this fails, what does it say about us?" She carried the strain, convinced that their loyalty would be honoured.

The Nova Team constantly buzzed around as if they were in a positive loop. But in reality, they were just minting every detail possible to safeguard themselves if they were to be exposed.

Once the work was complete, deflation crept in. Nova's tone shifted, masking intent.

Promises replaced payments. "We are waiting on investor disbursement."

"Thank you for your patience. We assure the payment will be cleared soon."

These excuses were convenient shields for Nova's team. On the contrary, for the Betelgeuse Team, each delay chipped away at morale until hope thinned into resentment.

Demeter refused to wait for stars that would never quite align.

She documented every exchange, compiled proof of deliverables, and rallied her team around action instead of waiting.

Legal notices followed, paired with industry whispers that made Nova's silencc costly.

Demeter mailed the Nova Studios with a clear message, Thank you for your ignorance. We assure that a legal follow-up will reach you soon."

Luna and Aster, once so eloquent, grew defensive under scrutiny.

Eventually, the agency's persistence forced Nova to settle - late, reluctant, but public enough to restore Betelgeuse's standing.

Demeter showed the agency and the world that justice meant setting boundaries and reclaiming dignity and not letting the perpetual victims buy authority.

Flippin' the Mirror (Self-Reflection)

We often chase the FLY in the room, blind to the one nesting in our own habits.

- How often do we ask for "just a little help" without clarifying intent?
- How often do we consume others' energy under the guise of collaboration, only to walk away when it suits us?

At times, the temptation to take shortcuts or lean on someone's brilliance without acknowledgement feels harmless, until we realise it mirrors the very behaviour we resent.

Every FLY that gets through the cracks often has help from us.

Not out of ignorance, but out of intention. The sheer human emotion of believing in the potential of a new partnership, the hope that generosity will return as loyalty, and the assumption that showing up early and offering more will be met with equal enthusiasm.

Sometimes, the doors we leave open by being overly generous, too available, or blindly optimistic invite more extraction than exchange.

Clarity begins by asking: *Am I truly contributing, or am I consuming?*

Your Space

The FLY teaches us to examine how freely we portray our kindness, to whom we portray it. Sometimes, our kindness becomes an invisible shield for the fly, backfiring on us when our actions are misconstrued as something we never intended. This truth is not to accuse, but to awaken.

Use these prompts to recognise when you have played the FLY or when you have let one play you:

- When have I taken more than I gave in for work?
- What patterns make me ignore red flags and keep giving?
- Have I ever used someone's ideas without acknowledgement? What was the justification?
- When did I stay silent while feeling drained or exploited after certain conversations?
- Do I mistake "relationship building" for free consulting – whether asking or allowing it?
- What boundaries can I create to stop myself from becoming, or enabling, a FLY?

It is always better to remind oneself that you do not owe your energy to those who borrowed your luminous limelight and never returned the favour.

The FLY feeds on what is left open, shut the sweetness before it is stolen!

CHAPTER 2

THE TERMITE
SILENTLY SABOTAGING YOU

The Subtle Decay

"Finally, someone dependable," whispered Agatha, Fund Manager for the Sovereign Crest Trust Fund, Zurich, seeing Arnold, who was joining as one of the "Trustees".

At first glance, Arnold appeared to be a remarkable asset as his professional profile looked immaculate.

Composed, soft-spoken, and perceptive, he exuded the aura of someone who had navigated challenges and emerged with wisdom, and his contributions in meetings were both measured and articulate. He never boasted, delivered documents on time, and always had thoughtful input.

He did not seek the limelight; instead, he cultivated trust through his low-maintenance approach. The board felt lucky.

However, as execution unfolded, a different narrative emerged. And then, the cracks appeared.

As deadlines loomed, Arnold would subtly withdraw.

He never vanished entirely but drifted just out of reach, delayed responses here, incomplete tasks there.

The message went unanswered for hours, then days.

Documents arrived half-signed.

Yet in confrontation, his words carried the sweetness of Lindt chocolates, the sheen of the Alps' snow, and the secrecy of Swiss banks.

"Arnold, where is the final deal and sealed document? It was supposed to be presented yesterday," asked Yuna, one of the board members, trying to keep calm.

Arnold smiled softly. "I did not want to rush and compromise on the deal. We have always valued authenticity. I am just making sure we live up to it." His tone conveyed no irritation, no excuses - only poise, which afforded him time.

The board exchanged looks. And in that moment, guilt shifted onto them. Maybe they were rushing him? Maybe it was their fault.

Gradually, the burden shifted.

Agatha went beyond his fund management duties, whereas Yuna and other Board Members absorbed his responsibilities, quietly managing the accumulating workload. Arnold never rejected accountability; he merely failed to follow through with his foggy presence.

In one meeting, Yuna's patience cracked. "Arnold, do you realise we are carrying your load?" Arnold gently shrugged and said, "I only thought we were a team… that you trusted me to take my time. If I have let you down, please know I feel bad about it." But there was no resistance, no apology. No denial, no resolution.

That was the moment the board understood:

Arnold was Kafka's Ghost, polite, present, but perpetually allowing the work to wither imperceptibly.

The invisible gnawing by the TERMITE had left the board members cracked and the Trust Fund to decay.

The Anatomy of a Rattler

In many organisations, the TERMITE personality initially appears as a quiet asset, accomplished, insightful, and eloquent, earning trust without seeking limelight. However, their engagement is often superficial and their contributions minimal. They express commitment but fail to deliver, typically citing personal challenges or sham scenes. These explanations, while plausible, deflect scrutiny, and their sporadic communication is easily mistaken for composure. People with these personalities tend to build up gradually, ultimately making a striking, cynical impact on the work environment and its beings.

The Corporate Jungle Where They Thrive

TERMITE personalities thrive in every stratum of the corporate world, from entry-level corridors to executive suites. Their ideal environment is one where oversight is infrequent, roles are vague, and accountability dissolves into the atmosphere like humidity, allowing small compromises to go unnoticed until the damage becomes irreversible.

- On the ground floor, they blend seamlessly with the swarm, difficult to detect and even harder to identify, gradually influencing processes and relationships.
- In higher ranks, they operate behind the facade of authority, disguising their self-serving instincts with polished presentations and strategic diplomacy.

What makes them formidable is their perseverance; they dismantle from within, grain by grain, while appearing indispensable to the very structures they weaken. Rarely confrontational, they cultivate networks of silent allies, creating a veneer of normalcy amid decay.

To outsiders, they seem adaptable; to those who see clearly, they are survivalists who have turned subtle erosion into an art form.

The Inaction Ick-Er

For a year, Loop & Live, the Miami media firm, ran like clockwork. The team met expectations, and the client was satisfied, maintaining a predictable and profitable monthly service routine.

Until the Annual Audit began.

Addie and Brady, the firm's co-founders, discovered the revenue gap.

Addie's eyes widened.

"Brady, where is the revenue for Infi-Night & Light?

Twelve months, nothing billed."

Brady frowned. "System glitch? Finance Team?"

They sought clarity from finance, but silence ensued.

No one had raised the invoice, tracked the workflow, or followed up. Each person assumed someone else was responsible. Just a "Loophole".

All fingers pointed to Toby, the Finance Executive, the man famous for his promising calm control.

Addie remembered his words, "I will do a follow-up."

Initially, one email was duly sent. Later, nothing.

In the debrief, Addie asked, "Toby, why was the invoice not raised?"

Toby eased back, tone laid-back as Miami nights. "I assumed you both wanted to keep the client relationship smooth. Chasing invoices too hard would have added sourness. So, I held off, thinking it was the strategic choice. If that were not aligned, then yes, probably, I would bestow the blame on myself."

His words dripped with courtesy but shifted weight onto them, as if they forgot that client trust mattered most.

This was a quiet failure of responsibility.

Vendor payments were delayed, not due to conflict, but from a lack of follow-through by someone capable. The victim was the firm's foundation - profits eaten away. The survivors were co-founders, scrambling to patch what had hollowed out.

And the perpetrator? Toby. The silent violator.

The Focus Fraud

Mel stared at thirteen tabs. How to Finish What You Start? But none inspired her. Instead, she sharpened her eyeliner, readying her armour.

As founder of Burn Theory, she drew clients in with mantras like "Let pain fund your comeback" and "Bleed but build." After sessions, they whispered,

"Mel, you saved us. We are back in the real sense, only because of you."

She would smile and say, "Discipline is devotion." But behind her desk, she drifted.

She spoke in timelines and to-do lists. Taught others to focus like warriors. But her hours slipped by shiny, formless, impossible to hold.

Every ritual she preached, she skipped. Every breakthrough she mapped, she avoided.

"Mel, when will you finish shooting the scheduled content?" her assistant asked gently. "Soon. I am refining the vision," she claimed.

Mel's ambition was trapped by instability while her carefully maintained brand thrived.

Mel's ambition was trapped by instability while her carefully maintained brand thrived.

Her downfall was not loud. It was knowing what to do and doing nothing.

Mel seemed neat while selling combustion, but inside, she was eroding.

Burn Theory looked lit while it caved silently.

Clean Jungle, Happy Culture

A healthy workplace transcends mere talent; it relies on structural integrity, and contributions are recognised, valued, and amplified. When this foundation quietly deteriorates, teams may seem intact but risk internal grinding, just like Gatsby's smile.

- Subtle behaviours, such as forgotten emails, missed deadlines, and uncommunicated shifts in responsibility, accumulate insidiously. This gradual decline undermines the trust that binds the team.
- Over time, proximity to these patterns dulls instincts, leading to second-guessing, withheld ideas, and decreased initiative.
- Momentum wanes due to a lack of follow-through.

Pattern Recognition, Not Paranoia

The TERMITE's weapon is to silently rewrite rules around you instead of completely breaking them.

Here are the patterns that reveal if you are battling on a TERMITE rattle ground:

- **Silent Emitters:** They do not voice concerns when it counts. Risks go unmentioned, and everyone else bears the impact.
- **Head-Nod Heroes:** They appear agreeable but miss deadlines, using "yes" as a performance while you cover their lapses.
- **Detail Withholders:** Key facts are selectively shared, forcing others to chase missing information they control.

- **Burden Shifters:** Tasks and accountability are redirected or dropped, with others left to pick up the pieces while they seem supportive.
- **Project Drifters:** Ambiguity causes deadlines to be missed and initiatives to halt, enabling small problems to escalate while maintaining an image of indispensability.

Dealing With the "Drama" Without any Drama

The only way to expose a TERMITE is with light.

Transparency removes their hiding spots.

When every task has a clear owner and deadline tracked openly in shared tools, its invisibility disappears. What once got buried in endless threads is now out in the open.

However, transparency alone is not enough; real accountability exists when delays have tangible consequences.

TERMITES thrive where there is no cost to procrastination. When missed deadlines impact performance reviews, bonuses, or how leaders perceive someone, avoiding accountability becomes risky.

Consistency is also essential. Progress checks should not fall post-harm is done; they should be routine. Openly asking, "*Why is this delayed?*" keeps steady pressure. This way, bottlenecks are identified early, and TERMITEs lose their shield of silence.

Yet, fairness calls for a final warning: *"Your delays are causing compliance fines and eroding vendor trust. We need to change by a set deadline, or responsibility will shift."* A one-on-one conversation should make the stakes clear, either to improve or step aside.

Many TERMITEs are long-tenured and protected by loyalty. But shielding a weak link undermines everyone else's morale and loyalty. A slow worker does not just delay projects but also weakens the entire organisation. Detachment from these personalities is and feels ruthless, but sometimes it is the only way to save the house from collapse.

The Commitment Ghost

Sage shoved the thick file across the desk.

His voice cracked with urgency. "Rita, the court date is in three days.

If this does not get filed, I lose everything - my business, my future, my name."

Rita replied, unruffled.

"Sage, trust me. Good work is God's work. Rushing ruins results. You will thank mc later for being thorough and leaving no room for flaws."

Rita had a presence that could be felt before it was understood.

At Legal Roots Advisory & Co., she became the operational glue behind the scenes.

She anticipated needs and smiled through challenges, speaking as if solutions were already in hand.

She held her ground by how she said yes and not by saying no.

Sage's chest tightened. Her words felt soothing, but the confusion stung.

Behind her composed smile, Rita's inner monologue hummed: Oh God, what is the rush? My value cannot be hurried. And he is in need here; he has nowhere to go. Only my name can make him win."

Here, sabotage was not overt; it was masqueraded as soft but strong assurance.

When Rita burrowed herself deep in her delusion, that is when Sage's wisdom lit up, bringing his name to action. He had to provoke her. He slammed his hand on the table and, in a soft yet strong voice, he said, "Rita, this is not about appearances. This is about survival. If you cannot act, I will find someone who will," striking an anti-termite treatment against her hidden rot.

For once, Rita's smile lines disappeared, and frown lines on her forehead popped out. Silence, her shield, cracked. That noon, Sage made sure that Rita called contacts, drafted motions, and created a strong case for him. He traded shame for action.

In court, the papers were filed, and the verdict tipped his way. Relief flooded in, but so did clarity.

Sage, unflinching like a Terminator, saw beyond Rita's composed facade and neutralised the termite threat at its roots.

Flippin' The Mirror (Self-Reflection)

The uncomfortable reality of becoming a TERMITE is that it scarcely appears malicious from within. You convince yourself you are merely "thinking it through," yet overthinking gradually undermines your momentum. Each delay weakens the structural integrity of the career and can reflect a neglect of self-potential. If left unchecked, it can compromise not just deliverables but also invade personal life, transforming ambition into anxiety and opportunity into regret.

Wole Soyinka aptly wrote, ***"The man dies in all who keep silent in the face of tyranny."***

In the workplace, this tyranny can be self-imposed, manifesting as a slow erosion of confidence when hesitation dominates action.

Often, you may not realise you have halted progress; instead, you have perfected the art of postponement.

Your Space

Every structure, whether of wood or trust, falls not to earthquakes but to what gnaws unseen. Termites in a workplace work the same way; they silently dismantle. The greatest defence is ruthless visibility: no shadows, no excuses. The moment there is a feeling of the first splinter of doubt, act. A single decisive move can save years of future ruin.

Use these prompts to recognise if you have been nibbled by a TERMITE or been a nibbler yourself:

- Where have I delayed under the excuse of "quality" when it was really avoidance?
- What silent habits of mine slowly shift burdens onto others?
- If my work were inspected grain by grain, what would collapse?
- Where have I granted too much benefit of the doubt, only to carry the hidden weight?
- Which tasks around me always feel "foggy" or unfinished, and who benefits from that fog?
- If I stopped covering for others, what accountability would surface?

Delays and decay both bring blockages in your personal and professional growth. A timely and authentic work ethic will guard you in all ways, always, as covering up the blockages at a later stage becomes knackering with a multiplied cost.

Termites only thrive where wood is soft and hidden. Sharpen your edges, illuminate the cracks, and do not feed decay with silence or indulgence.

CHAPTER 3

THE DONKEY STANDING STILL

The Quantum of Quantara

"*This place would collapse without me,*" Keren claimed one Monday, dropping files with a theatrical flair. Caught between the awkward drama, the receptionist smiled cautiously.

Keren had worked in *Human Resources at Quantara* so long that she saw herself as the office's beast of burden.

Though her badge read *"Senior Trainer,"* her stubbornness, loud sighs, and tireless routines dominated the corridors.

She bustled through the office, phone at her ear, convinced everything relied on her relentless effort, and made sure everyone knew it.

By lunch, Keren was already braying about her latest ordeal. *"Had to redo the entire orientation. Someone sent a guy who could barely speak. Nobody does any real work here."* Her audience chuckled, out of habit; few dared disagree with her balky assertions.

Across the cafeteria, *Ari*, the intern, replayed Keren's orientation, the clipped commands, dismissive eyerolls, and that unmistakable, impatient *"Next slide!"* that trampled over any question. *"I only asked about leave policy,"* Ari told a colleague. Keren quipped, *'You think you are on vacation?'* She looked around the empty office and smiled wryly.

This, she thought, is corporate training: where the *"Kerens" outlast the kind.* That night, Ari typed an email she would never send:

Dear Keren, thanks for proving confusion as a crime. Next time, I will Google my way to belonging.

Meanwhile, Keren ended her day with a satisfied sigh. In her mind, she was the Quantum of the Quantara, the one who pulled the load that everyone else abandoned. She would often quote, *"If you want the cart to move, you need someone strong (stubborn) enough to keep pulling, no matter how noisy the road is."*

And others would often fall prey to her brays.

The Anatomy of a Bray

The DONKEY personality symbolises those who are reliable and diligent, yet deeply resistant to change.

- Not all interruptions to progress come from negative intent; sometimes, they stem from a strong attachment to tradition.
- Rooted in routine and anchored by years of experience, they follow familiar and comfortable paths with sustained loyalty, knowing better roads lie ahead.
- Their strength lies in stability, but that very trait becomes a barrier when evolution is needed.

DONKEYS will not oppose change out of spite; they simply trust what has always been.

However, in environments that demand agility, their steadfastness can quietly stall growth and stifle possibility.

The Corporate Jungle Where they Thrive

Within systems, DONKEY-type personalities are the institutional anchors - dependable, unshakable.

- They are usually seen in legacy roles: operations, compliance, or department leads who have been around since the "beginning".
- They prosper in systems that mistake consistency for competence, where the comfort of *"how it has always been done"* outweighs the urgency of change.

These personalities dream of hiking across mountains but tend to forget that they are the ones curbing their own feet. Their stubbornness is rarely challenged because it is cloaked in years of service and titles that earn them reverence. This reverence without renewal leads to rot. They will not resist with aggression, but with reassurance. Every suggestion would be met with a cautionary tale; every spark of innovation smothered under layers of precedent. The danger is not in what they oppose, but in how they stall everything around them.

Ray, The Bossy Boss

"Cloud, cloud, cloud," Ray grumbled like an uprising storm.

"I have balanced these books longer than that system's been here."

With a tenure that predates even the air conditioner, Ray has been holding his coordinates for fifteen years with the same desk and the same latitude of loyalty at Meridian Axis Ltd. When it comes to the company's ledgers and numbers, Ray's familiarity rivals the company directory (and unlike the air conditioner, he never needs a reboot).

The company began transitioning to a cloud-based accounting system, and younger team members welcomed this change as it promised to reduce manual work and minimise errors.

"Who changed my formulas again?" Ray's voice cut through the office. Heads looked up, startled. Ray stood at his cluttered desk, fidgeting with his pen, and frustration on his face.

"Ray, it is the new system update. The cloud auto-syncs everything now." Maya, the Junior Analyst, anxiously replied. Maya tried helping, but Ray had already returned to his screen, determined to repair the unbroken, sticking to his trusted spreadsheets, often delegating tasks in fragments, and holding critical information close. Brushing aside tutorials and training sessions of the new systems and repeated encouragement from managers and peers, Ray refused to adapt. The Meridian Axis felt flat.

Over time, what used to be respect began to feel like avoidance.

Teammates hesitated to question him.

Discrepancies crept in, and the workflow slowed down.

Though no one said it outright, a quiet tension settled in the room.

One evening, as Maya packed up, she saw Ray in the monitor's blue glow - exhausted.

She thought, maybe this is how it begins. You try to save the system, then become the system no one can change. She saw the stubbornness she feared in herself.

Ray did not mean harm; he simply believed his way still worked the best.

Yet his insistence on preserving the past paused the future.

Breaking Bad With Elon & Mickey

The meeting started five minutes late. Not that either mentioned it. Elon, the seasoned retailer, adjusted his camera, smirking. "Ah, finally. I was beginning to think startups run on startup time." Mickey, the scrupulous startup founder, smiled back, civil and courteous. "Only when the client reads the brief on time."

A pause. Heavy enough to echo.

On-screen, the prototype loaded - fluid, minimal, proud of its youth. "Though my customers are not exactly Gen-Z, this is surely an interesting layout," Elon said. Mickey replied, "Absolutely. But they might need a reason to stay beyond nostalgia."

"Legacy sells, Mickey. It always has." Elon's lips twitched, saying so. Mickey's cursor hovered mid-air, slightly annoyed, "Until it stops clicking." They both laughed off lightly, precisely two seconds long, maintaining professional decorum.

Weeks turned into polite chaos. Revisions circled back like déjà vu. Elon believed the platform was too rigid. Mickey thought Elon was too stuck in the past. "Almost there," Elon would write. "Almost aligned," Mickey replied.

Neither adapted nor did they understand each other.

Elon believed the platform was too rigid.

Mickey thought Elon was too stuck in the past.

Neither adapted, and eventually, Elon backed out, claiming he would build something in-house. For him, his pride of being a visionary took over. Mickey thought they still mistook control for wisdom and, without flinching, said, "That is probably best. Innovation struggles when it needs permission."

In truth, they were two tectonic plates: firm in direction, rich in substance, but unwilling to bend.

When they brushed, friction sparked. If they clashed, a quake was inevitable.

But had they moved in rhythm, side by side, they might have shaped something sustainable, maybe even seismic in its strength.

But alas! Two donkeys shared a dream;
the cart never left the barn.

Clean Jungle, Happy Culture

DONKEY personalities, defined by rigidity and resistance to change, act as invisible anchors in organisations. Their reluctance to adapt or listen inhibits innovation, hinders collaboration, and weakens morale. Even the most talented teams can feel trapped under the weight of their certainty, slowing decisions and fracturing trust.

Recognising and consciously managing these dynamics helps organisations address friction, promote coexistence, prevent stagnation, foster creativity, and ultimately support growth for individuals, teams, and institutions alike.

Pattern Recognition, Not Paranoia

Slow and steady does not always win; sometimes, they just block the path.

Here is how you can identify the path blockers:

- **Defiance Diggers:** They choose the familiar 'wrong way' over the unfamiliar right way. Firm, but not loud, they disguise their fear of uncertainty as discipline, presenting inertia as wisdom.
- **Mock Managers:** "*I will take care of it*" sounds dependable. In reality, complexity becomes their defence. They stall, flag every risk, and let others take over out of exhaustion.
- **Seasoned Stallers:** Innovative ideas often meet hesitation with a pause, a frown, and a softly spoken, "*Hmm, we can think about that.*" Resistance is presented with logic, making obstruction seem thoughtful and deliberate.

- **Compliance Guardians:** They safeguard comfort and procedure instead of admitting gaps or flaws. The status quo becomes untouchable, even when broken.
- **Subtle Manipulators:** They are defined by their control without true commitment. By steering work indirectly, they create friction yet continue to project an image of diligence.

Dealing With The "Drama" Without Any Drama

A DONKEY personality is driven by a deep need for certainty and the fear of being irrelevant; hence, the resistance is expressed.

Fighting a DONKEY with force only makes them dig their heels deeper. The more you push, the stronger their grip on their conventionality becomes. Instead of escalating, pause.

- Stubbornness feeds on confrontation. So, the real key is not to overpower them but to reframe change as continuity. Propose transitions instead of announcing a revolution.
- Offer options that feel safe, familiar, and grounded in logic. Let evolution feel like reinforcement, not replacement.

Dealing with these personality types requires diplomacy. Language is the greatest tool to tether abstractions to their existing structure. "*Let us run a small pilot alongside what's working*", invites curiosity, whereas "*Let us change everything*" might spark panic. Using data, drawing parallels, and most importantly, acknowledging their experience will validate their foundation, and they will willingly try to build on it. This is not manipulation; it is design thinking applied to people.

DONKEYS only move when they feel seen, respected, and secure, not when pushed.

While it can take time to reach your destination with a DONKEY, the journey is worthwhile. When a DONKEY chooses to walk by your side, no terrain is too challenging. That calm fortitude is their superpower.

From Surviving to Thriving

The air inside Sutra Textiles carried a faint hum of the looms and legacy. Threads in turmeric, maroon, and indigo frolicking across the wooden frames, each spool spinning stories older than its workers. Morning light filtered through dusty glass panes, glinting off rolls of silk that had once dressed queens and weddings alike.

Shashi loved the rhythmic, predictable, and loyal pattern of Surat's (A city situated in the Indian State of Gujarat) best, Sutra Textiles, which he had built brick by brick, thread by thread.

At the far end of the factory floor, Ria walked in wearing a linen suit, a laptop bag, and a whiff of the world beyond Surat.

Freshly back from London Business School, she saw untapped potential.

With global trends leaning into heritage fabrics and sustainable fashion, she proposed a rebrand with a digital storefront and influencer tie-ins.

"Paa, we are sitting on a goldmine of legacy; let us make it modern and global," she said.

Shashi peered over his glasses, half-amused, half-wary. He replied dismissively, "They get to see it when they are here to buy it. Marketing is just noise. Only the handwork and hard work counts.".

That night, Ria shared a single reel, casually with courage: a gentle, behind-the-scenes clip of a weaver's fingers weaving the loom, captioned, "Woven by time, with love." The video quickly went viral, with inquiries arriving from Brazil, Morocco, Singapore, London, to Ibiza. Ria's phone buzzed nonstop. Shashi did not. He scrolled once, frowned, and muttered, "Internet people are just browsers, not buyers."

But they did buy. So, Ria kept posting the pride, not just promotions. Behind-the-scenes moments. Weavers smiling. Clients unboxing and testimonials.

Months later, at the half-yearly review, Ria was ready with fabric swatches tagged with new clients' names. She excitedly announced,

"The story sells, Paa, because people buy emotion before they buy silk. Online sales were up by 40%, but walk-ins had grown too. They come in saying they saw us digitally.

Your legacy still pulls them in. I just built the bridge."

And in that moment, he saw "change" as a renewal, not rebellion.

Shashi was stunned to see the numbers, and he kept scanning through them. He did not reply at once. The clock ticked. The looms kept singing. Finally, in a hushed tone, he said, "Just do not lose the old buyers chasing the new ones."

She smiled. "I will weave them both in." Gradually, Sutra became a soft global whisper in the sustainable fashion circle.

This time, the DONKEY in Shashi stayed on the path. Only this time, the route redirected somewhere new and better.

Flippin' The Mirror (Self-Reflection)

Change can be daunting, yet it is an inevitable part of life. Each of us harbours a "DONKEY" within, a tendency to cling to the familiar, not from strength but from quiet fear. This may manifest as resistance to new systems because the old ones "still work" or dismissing younger colleagues' insights, mistakenly believing that experience outweighs fresh perspectives. Such moments, though they may seem philosophical, often reflect comfort disguised as conviction.

True reflection involves confronting tough questions:

- *Am I fostering value or hindering growth?*
- *Is my hesitation a thoughtful consideration or a territorial instinct?*
- *In the pursuit of perfection, have I lost my curiosity?*

Maturity does not stem from tenure but from a willingness to question and explore. Stubbornness may feel like steadfastness, but when progress halts, we become ensnared in chaos. Ultimately, DONKEYS must choose to move forward, lest they be left behind in an ever-evolving world.

YOUR SPACE

Rumi wisely stated, "*Do not get lost in your pain. Know that one day your pain will become your cure.*"

This wisdom applies equally to institutions and individuals. Personalities that resist change can, with proper guidance, become strong advocates for it. Rather than silencing the DONKEY, we should harness its strength for progress, making sure that forward movement is experienced, not just recalled.

Use these prompts to recognise if you have been kicked by a DONKEY or been a kicker yourself:

- What aspect of my work or identity do I protect so fiercely that any change feels threatening, rather than like an opportunity for growth? (Reflect on the fears underlying this rigidity.)
- Can I recall a time when I resisted a new idea? Was that resistance rooted in genuine wisdom, or was it worry disguised as wisdom?
- Is there a "responsibility" I have held onto for so long it defines my worth, even though it might actually be limiting me?
- Think of a time when someone's inflexibility hindered progress. How did their stubbornness affect you? Did it cause you to shrink, pause, or adapt?
- When faced with stubborn people, do you tend to push harder, wait them out, or walk away? What drives your typical response?
- What has interacting with a "DONKEY" personality taught you about patience, persuasion, or setting boundaries that pure logic never could?

There is a fine line between standing firm and standing still. The Donkey lives right there until you move it.

CHAPTER 4

THE CUCKOO
STEALING & HATCHING YOUR STORIES

The Glorification of Grief

"You will make it big someday," Tori used to tell her. Covvey would giddily smile and say, "We both shall."

Covvey, a rising social media star, possessed a glow that made people pause mid-scroll with her melodic face and mellow voice. She carried herself with full pride, even though she was not yet famous.

Her life appeared to be a carefully crafted dream with posts that felt therapeutic and captions straight out of classic literature.

Tori, her neighbour, classmate, and best friend from childhood, and by profession an Artist Manager, knew her long before the days of filters and followers, back when ambitions were expressed in doodles and scribbles rather than in edited reels.

They both grew together. Tori supported her through creative blocks, heartbreaks, algorithm dips, never seeking credit, always cheering behind the scenes.

Tori was the anchor; Covvey was the wind.

Until the applause got louder, for only one of them.

Gradually, conversations tilted towards Covvey: her content calendar, her collabs, her anxieties about "staying relevant." "What do you think of this caption?" Covvey asked, not pausing for a response. "It is nice, but it sounds familiar." Tori would reply with her eyebrows and doubts raised.

Weeks later, while doom-scrolling, Tori froze, seeing a carousel post of the very memory she had confronted with Covvey with tears, now story titled 'In the Wake of What Was.'

Her words and grief - Glorified.

There was no mention, no context of her, just borrowed truth rebranded and launched as personal growth.

Tori squared up to Covvey, saying, "It was not your story to publicise."

Covvey, without making eye contact in a sedated manner, responded, "Everything is a story if you frame and sing it well. I thought you would be proud that the story is helping people, and me, your best friend, is finally getting the needed social spark."

Tori felt the room and her heart shrink. Fortunately(un), Tori realised that not everyone enters your life to grow alongside you; some come into your life to find their own growth through you. It was clear that Covvey did not want to be friends anymore. She just wanted a platform to perform.

She was willing to nest in someone else's life to build her own.

The Anatomy of a Coo

The CUCKOO personality, polished, precise, and attentive, forms quick connections, aligning with what already exists.

A friend with influence, a colleague with momentum, a partner with presence, they know where and how to land. Initially, they offer insight and support, but over time, roles shift; personal stories are echoed elsewhere, and ideas reappear in someone else's voice. The energy flows predominantly in one direction.

- In nature, the CUCKOO lays its eggs in another bird's nest, often that of a crow.
- The host raises what is not theirs, oblivious to the cost until it is too late.

This pattern mirrors the actions of CUCKOO-type people: When the nest is finally emptied of your time, your truth, your tenderness, those you nurtured take flight, and all that is left is a silence where there was once song.

The Corporate Jungle where they Thrive

CUCKOO-type people are found in fluid environments with ambiguous roles where credit is loosely shared.

- These individuals excel at positioning themselves strategically to ensure they are indispensable without creating disruption.
- These personalities have a knack for slipping into established systems just when the groundwork has been laid, avoiding the initial chaos of early project stages.
- They thrive in settings where emotional labour is invisible and results are hard to quantify, advancing through proximity rather than performance, quietly borrowing energy, language, and trust from those around them. They operate in that elusive middle layer, visible and valuable yet seldom held accountable.

Over time, CUCKOO personalities find their niche with an instinct for observation; they study those who are capable, consistent, and emotionally available, aligning themselves closely to leverage their strengths. Their presence can morph into mere echoes of others' brilliance, and what might appear as a partnership slowly turns into dependence.

The Hive Heist

Beneath Damalis' gentle demeanour lay a well-crafted plan.

At Buzzover's Indian Hive, Damalis, Assistant Supply Chain Manager, was renowned for his low-volume, high-frequency vibes. Often, he brought homemade herbal drinks mixed with the company's top-selling Manuka Honey and a dose of his enticing sweetness to meetings.

He often stayed late "just to help." He frequently discussed burnout, not his own, but that of others. He remembered minute details and followed up on personal struggles.

"How is your mum's health, Parul?"

"Still swamped with single dad duties, Aryan?"

This felt thoughtful and made people open up. Also, disarming.

With every conversation, a new story about him emerged: he was the helpful colleague, the quiet glue, the one who held the team together. One night, while leaving the office premises, in a casual conversation, Damalis began, "I sometimes worry I am holding the team back. While it is flattering to be relied on, perhaps I would thrive more in a place where leadership fully utilises my potential and allows me to move things forward faster." Aryan promptly replied, "You? Holding us back? Truthfully, you are the King-Bee of this hive." and tittered, unaware of validating Damalis' exit plan.

Damalis had set his sights on the Tanzanian Hive, a smaller unit, characterised by newer leadership and swifter paths to promotion.

He began to insinuate that he might be "better suited elsewhere," proposing that his skills could have a greater impact in evolving environments.

He solicited anonymous 360° feedback from teammates and highlighted team victories in global meetings, always positioning himself subtly at the centre. Weeks later, this narrative propelled him forward. His account of selfless contribution facilitated a seamless transfer.

The Tanzanian Hive embraced him as a burgeoning changemaker.

He smiled modestly. Cunningly.

The team celebrated, mistaking loss for pride. After his transfer, the Indian Hive was left in his wake with disrupted workflows, diminished morale, and a quiet sense of loss, though no one could quite articulate it. Aryan caught himself saying, "We just need someone like Damalis again." He paused, coming to terms with the bitter reality that he had made them rely on him.

Such is the genius of the CUCKOO.
Nothing is taken outright; it is inherited.

The Nest of Narrative

"Your grief… it is divine," Cyra cooed.

Cyra, 22, is a self-proclaimed manifestation coach with 108k followers and no credentials, backed by only her shine. Her bio read: "Quantum Energy Alchemist | Inner Child Healer | Billionaire Mindset Coach." Her pinned reel, titled "Rewire Your Abundance Frequency in 11 Hours," had 3.3 million views.

Sixteen-year-old Trinette joined Cyra's live session. College, parental fights, endless nights of tears. She clung to her pillow in the hope that someone, somewhere, understood her. "It feels as if my soul is breaking apart.

How did you manage to become so strong?"

Trinette put up her question in the live chat.

Visibly, everyone could see that Cyra's confident aura wavered. For a fraction of a second, her smile flickered. "I… uh…" Cyra hesitated, then smiled again, softer this time. How do I answer this? "By feeling… deeply. By connecting."

Trinette's innocent heart never quite comprehended the complexity behind Cyra's words, yet she never questioned them. As a devoted fan, she placed her trust in every syllable, every mantra, every manifestation ritual. In tough moments, she would replay those words, holding on to them as if they were her lifeline.

Truth be told, Cyra never engaged in outright deception; that was her genius.

She had never experienced heartbreak, yet she led grief workshops.

Though she had never known scarcity, she sold digital money spells.

Despite not having healed herself, she taught thousands how to "transcend trauma."

Cyra's brand epitomised a unique fusion of curated emotional experiences, the depths of internet confessions, TikTok narratives, and Reddit threads. This emotional mimicry was expertly, cosmetically, or here "cosmologically" altered as spiritual guidance with rose quartz filters, lo-fi soundscapes, and poignant captions. Rather than guiding her audience towards self-discovery or genuine healing, she led them into an emotionally engineered maze and a commoditised hope.

In their most vulnerable moments, her followers often confused her performance for authentic peace and a universe's sign.

In a world where pain is turned into profit and branding turns into belief, CUCKOOS sing loud and proud, "Wear their wounds like wings".

Clean Jungle, Happy Culture

Some beginnings hum like healing and end in hollow.

CUCKOO-type personalities distort systems with their sweet songs.

- What gets lost is harder to measure: confidence, creative momentum, and psychological safety.
- People start withholding ideas.

- Meetings feel performative.
- Credit gets cloudy.
- Over time, teams spend more energy managing emotional weight than doing meaningful work.

A healthy workplace does not avoid conflict; it does not confuse manipulation with contribution.

When clarity is protected, and emotional labour is not exploited, teams operate at full capacity.

Getting rid of the CUCKOO should be about realignment, not exile.

Pattern Recognition, Not Paranoia

The Cuckoo's Calling (a Novel by J.K. Rowling) reminds us that not every voice that echoes back is what it seems. Sometimes, the wisdom lies not in what is said, but in who sings the story, and where they first heard it.

CUCKOO-type personalities rarely disclose themselves through overt actions; when they recur across different settings or relationships, they deserve to be registered with clarity and not suspicion.

Here are the signs of these sweet songbirds:

- **Selective Empaths:** The easiest indicator is their emotional asymmetry. Their crises frequently become the centre of gravity, even during others' moments of vulnerability or success; the focus discreetly shifts back to their tale. Over time, the experiences of those around them may begin to recede into the background.
- **Uneven Contributors:** Often, in personal relationships, professional collaborations, or emotional exchanges, a subtle imbalance develops: one party may invest more emotionally or practically than the other. This inequality is frequently masked by feelings of care, admiration, or a sense of shared purpose.

- **Boundary Breakers:** While influence is natural, parroting without boundaries can cross into subtle appropriation. When private experiences shared in confidence begin to surface, whether as snitched phrases, reflected anecdotes, or content subtly reflecting someone's life without acknowledgement, it may indicate a multilayered motif.

Dealing with the "Drama" without any Drama

CUCKOO personalities do not necessitate dramatic exits; rather, they require the removal of fertile ground. Without access to personal insight, blurred lines, or unearned support, their pattern cannot sustain itself.

Establishing defined roles, documented workflows, and clear deliverables restricts their capacity to extract value without accountability. Their influence often hinges on emotional positioning, framing needs as exceptional or urgent; thus, decisions must remain data-driven and outcome-focused.

Flattery or exaggerated emotional connection expressions like *"no one gets me like you do"* should not be misconstrued as trust but recognised as a tactic to deepen emotional dependency. Respond with neutrality rather than empathy.

When encountering mimicry or uncredited snaffle, resist the urge to correct or reclaim your work. Focus on evolving your own voice, techniques, and creations at a pace that imitation cannot keep up with.

Predominantly, do not anchor self-worth to their validation or volatility. Boundaries should be firm, quiet, and consistent. free from explanation or emotional charge. Minimise exclusive access and shift interactions to visible, structured environments where ambiguity holds less sway.

The Feathered Forecast

One Friday evening, while the trade was closing, one of the minds at *Merle*'s company alerted her about the client portfolio dips. "Maybe the planets and market were not aligned for the day". Merle made the statement with an air of nonchalance, yet remained mindful throughout.

Merle had always been magnetic. A top business school graduate with a portfolio sharper than her focus. She not just followed trends but inhaled them.

She pursued mentorships, MNCs, and moguls, until quiet rejection reframed her ambition: if she could not join power, she would emulate it.

At the *Echelon Investors' Brunch*, she slid into a stock debate with an easy smile. *"So, what if trading is not about data, just desire?"* she said lightly, eyes locked on their attention. Intrigued by her statement, even the most stoic analysts and tycoons leaned closer. She smiled as she had her Eureka Moment. That night, she dove into YouTube tutorials and scanned the internet as much as she could.

Within weeks, she was the founder of Compound Minds Ltd., a trading firm built on Pinterest-y branding and Tumblr language.

Her pitch? *"Disrupting retail investing with EQ & IQ."* She did not offer projections but presence. Dauntingly, she declared in public that she was here to count stories, not sums.

As the clocks ticked, Merle trademarked mantras, hosted panels, and landed on *Forbes 30 Under 30.* Investors were not backing the business; they were betting on her.

Among her early supporters were those very tycoons from the brunch, now partners in her rise.

Joining her wagon were First-time traders, legacy funders, and former colleagues followed, drawn in by the illusion of "pre-earned success".

Celebrating her success in her penthouse, she relaxed with a luxurious dinner party, city views, and fine champagne, her lips reciting softly, *"I am a kind and worthy boss. The world owes me for sharing my knowledge and skills. While most people work hard to get by, I make it easy for them to earn money. Their success stories are my success, too."* Mighty Merle had soared.

But behind the stellar delivery, there was no algorithm. No thesis. No edge. Just recycled jargon and second-hand insight.

She never scaled the business; she scaled around it.

Over time, the numbers exposed the truth as portfolios slipped. Defending herself, Merle would say, *"Volatility is part of the evolution,"* as if she bore no business for others' money.

Behind closed doors, the board documented everything. The projections she pitched were compiled from their private presentations but rebranded as her ideas. Weeks later, the boardroom was silent as a folder slid her way. "Your shares are being reallocated. Consider this... a rebalancing of energies." She was stunned, lips parted in disbelief, as their voices echoed her former charm.

Outside, Merle's followers kept sharing her entrepreneurship quotes. Inside, her empire was quietly reclaimed, portfolios and reputations restored.

Investors calmly took back what was theirs, a revenge even a cuckoo would respect.

Merle realised that the only stock she truly grew was social capital. Featherlight, but floatable.

Eventually, it too got its *dip*

Flippin' The Mirror (Self-Reflection)

Before addressing the CUCKOO in the room, it is worth considering: have we ever sung in someone else's voice? Language on loan, relied too heavily on other beings' emotional labour, or built momentum from stories that were not fully theirs to tell?

The CUCKOO is not always a villain; sometimes, it represents a phase like a shortcut taken during periods of self-doubt, survival, or ambition. Constructing one's own nest takes longer, but it is more sustainable because if the nest is not yours, neither is the peace.

Your Space

Rather than usurping your position, the CUCKOO silently slips into your quiet moments. They may not always deceive, but they certainly possess the subtle ability to supplant you within your own narrative. Amid a landscape saturated with imitation and emotional manipulation, true currency lies beyond reason: an authentic self, expressed in a single, persistent line. Safeguard your originality like you would your assets. Remember to always *guard your nest.*

Use these prompts to recognise if you have been captivated by a CUCKOO's song or been a captor yourself:

- When someone else's story began echoing louder than mine, did I mistake their volume for value or my silence for peace?
- Have I ever leaned so close to another person's healing that I forgot where my hurt began?
- If pieces of my pain now live in someone else's words, do I still recognise the voice as my own?
- When I copy-paste the pain of others to sound wiser, do I hear resonance? Or the hollowness inside my empathy?
- Have I learned to comfort or to curate, and at what point did my care become content?
- If applause fell silent, would my purpose still sing or would the nest I built collapse into quiet truth?

The nest might look bustling, but beware the cheeky CUCKOO: it waddles in, snatches your sweat and sparkle, then soars off, cackling with your glory, leaving feathers and empty eggshells behind.

Save your words, work, and your energies.

CHAPTER 5

THE OCTOPUS
THE PUPPETEER WITHOUT STRINGS

Entangled with an Octopus

It turns out, Allen had more arms than intentions.

At Fork & Fin, Sydney's premier fine dining establishment overlooking Darling Harbour, Allen was revered for his composure and command. As General Manager, he managed the restaurant like a quiet symphony, flawless in form, understated in flair. To guests, the experience was seamless. Behind the calm façade, however, the reality flowed like ink beneath still water.

Max and Carol, the two Operations Executives, had started making waves through synergy and showmanship. Their collaboration produced streamlined systems and glowing team feedback. They were certainly gaining more attention from the board. Even the regional director had remarked, "Whatever they are doing, bottle it."

That was the trigger moment. Allen found himself lingering in the boardroom longer than usual. He perceived what others overlooked; two minds merging into a single rising tide, a tandem force capable of altering the current he had carefully controlled and stabilised.

Collaboration could quickly turn to competition, and competition had no place under his reign.

It was then that Allen made his move. Not outwardly, but inwardly.

"Carol, you have instincts, I have rarely seen in anyone. Just do not let it be "MAX" -ed out by anyone. You know who I am referring to here."

Allen said, voice smooth as butter.

Later that evening with Max, it was: "Carol is brilliant, right. But I feel she is a little insecure. And for Leadership, you must take charge, not wait for your instincts to kick in."

He brought them into strategy calls, praised their instincts, and mentored them like a seasoned captain. Trust built steadily; they confided in him and valued his guidance.

Quiet recalibrations emerged: projects with undefined edges, praise that split the pair, and private feedback questioning their "dependence" with remarks like, "You two are quite the exclusive club, aren't you?" The term "exclusive" soon felt political. That narrative slowly permeated everything.

Carol soon received a leadership offer with better pay in Melbourne. She walked into Allen's office, letter in hand. "I cannot leave, you have invested so much in me.", she said, torn. Allen smiled, proud. "Loyalty is rare, Carol. The company notices."

Weeks later, Max was blindsided by a performance review citing "collaborative friction." "Is this about Carol?" he asked. Allen smiled, cunningly, "Let us just conclude that sometimes harmony requires recalibration".

Eventually, Carol & Max's rapport dimmed, ideas slowed, and silences replaced shared enthusiasm. And Allen got his subtle-gilded control.

The Anatomy of a Tentacle-R

OCTOPUS personalities are high-functioning, strategic individuals who possess glamour and social magnetism.

- By seeking access to your thoughts, relationships, and identity, these individuals envelop you in attention, making you feel special and chosen.
- They offer champagne when you expect water, fast-tracking your rise before you are grounded.
- You do not realise you are being managed under the name of an opportunity until you feel trapped.

It is not just manipulation; it is slow, invisible control that influences your decisions without awareness. Gradually, you filter your words, second-guess your instincts, and shrink inside a life that appears grand from the outside.

The Corporate Jungle where they Thrive

The tentacle beasts thrive in environments where performance is valued, visibility is mandatory, and boundaries are fluid.

The modern corporate world, with its shifting hierarchies and subtle power dynamics, provides them with access, ambiguity, and attention. Industries such as media, fashion, politics, hospitality, and high-end consulting offer the ideal setting. In these spaces, gravitas often overshadows character, and influence can outweigh consequences.

Their ambition appears as leadership, while their manipulation resembles mentorship.

Surrounded by admiration and competition, their methods often go unquestioned, especially when results are evident. They excel at shaping perspectives, cultivating solidarity through selective access, and blurring professional and personal boundaries.

The Damaged Daisy

From her seed bloomed meaning; from his shadow, moss. And slowly, her sunlight became his shade.

Serene, soft, realistic, and relatable content like this inspired a substantial number of beings to appreciate nature's essence. From a quaint Dutch town, *Daisy* reimagined floriculture as a poetic art form. Despite limited recognition, her originality was evident; each word stemmed from genuine experience, and every visual reflected her concern. She aimed to cultivate depth, not chase fame.

Then came *Henry*, an 'eco-brand consultant'. Bali-based, linen-shirted, and Bond-level suave. His content was slick but had plateaued. To rebrand his content, he was in search of some inspiration and randomly stumbled upon Daisy's page. Watching Daisy's world bloom effortlessly pricked something sharp inside him. He envied her softness. He had a wild thought of joining her content with his strategy to own the niche, overnight.

So, he messaged her. *"Daisy, your work shines like art beneath sunlight."* Flattered, Daisy replied, *"You make it profound."*

"Because it is. Let us work together. Your art deserves to be seen. Probably, I can help with a blueprint," he replied.

Flattery gradually gave way to subtle dominance, all disguised as collaboration.

He would often say, *"Unfortunately, people do judge a book by its cover. The content is there, but the structure feels unhinged."* And soon, the content was published out in the world on both of their accounts. Henry's feed was mirrored and marketed with Daisy's tone, textures, and metaphors, all tropical filtered. But only Henry became the face of "floral wellness." Daisy became the ghost behind the brand.

Time did what it always does.

Daisy's page was shadowed, collaborators drifted, and the algorithm crowned Henry king.

In a conversation, Daisy confronted, *"I feel like a puppet, Henry."* He pouted. *"Inspiration is not ownership, dear. Let us keep emotions out; it ruins brand value."*

She felt silenced in reclamation, not defeat. The *caption* that introduced Henry to her made sense, now.

The Motherly Silk

"Moira, after everything we have shared, would you really abandon the family?"

In the refined world of European cinema, the Menezes family was an institution, a graceful, old-moneyed, untouchable.

Their films won awards, and their legacy earned global admiration. At the centre was Isabella Menezes, the co-founder, matriarch, and quiet authority behind every major decision. She was famous for her poise, like poetry, and punctuation, like control.

Moira, a respected brand strategist, was invited to consult on Menezes Studios' digital revival. Isabella welcomed her warmly with an elaborate English Brunch Setup. As sunlight streamed through the villa windows, Moira felt recognised in a way that was rare and real as Isabella said, *"You remind me of who I was before the world expected me to be who I am."* For Moira, Isabella felt like a legacy, and her inclusion, an honour.

Soon, she was invited to family events, asked to mentor Isabella's niece. While Isabella handed notes to Moira, she said, "*You have dreamy eyes; unfortunately, they are getting blinded by the outer world. Pause other projects until the Menezes mission is whole."*

There were no contracts, only warmth and an unspoken belief that she belonged.

Gradually, her time, ideas, and energy became theirs.

Clients drifted.

Credits and boundaries faded.

Isabella viewed herself as the matriarch in Moira's life. She told herself, *"Without me, she is nothing. I gave Moira chances she never dreamed of. I built her life, so she owes me loyalty. If she feels trapped, it is because she is reliant on my care."*

Moira tried to leave tacitly, but encountered a wave of legal notices and then, silence.

Her work, still on display, now reworked and gilded, continued to speak for her. Once celebrated and supported, she found herself steadily becoming more isolated.

Despite being hurt, Moira chose never to address it publicly, knowing it was unwise to harm those who support, even if their motherly embrace feels like a suffocating grip.

Clean Jungle, Happy Culture

OCTOPUS personalities influence like silk over stone, easily monopolising credit and conversations. They lead with a present force but leave zero room for others to rise. This subtle dominance saps team energy, silences ideas, and shifts culture from vibrant to cautious. In the rapidly growing professional world where equality is worshipped, spotting/managing/getting rid of OCTOPUS becomes a need. To ensure a seamless workflow and preserve sanity at all levels, the OCTOPUS's dictatorship must be dismantled.

Pattern Recognition, Not Paranoia

These OCTOPUSES, unlike the friendly cartoon OSWALD, are not your allies; instead, they are masters at making you forget your solo swim.

Here is how to recognise a professional friend or foe:

- **Subtle Arc Shapers:** They use vague promises and closeness to influence you, not formal agreements. Eventually, you hesitate to pursue other opportunities, telling yourself, "Maybe they mean well," and unknowingly start meeting their expectations.
- **Credit Eroders:** Your ideas merge into a "shared vision," with contributions reworded until your ownership is unclear. In meetings, your voice fades and provided input feels like someone else's, leaving you unsure and insecure.
- **Doubt Builders:** Subtle cues prompt you to self-censor, leading you to edit your ideas before others intervene. Your confidence quietly erodes, causing you to doubt your instincts and decisions.
- **Exclusive Inviters:** Being chosen for inner circles creates a sense of privilege, distracting you from the gradual loss of independence that comes with such inclusion.
- **Emotional Cartographers:** They precisely read your vulnerabilities and desires, subtly steering your actions and fostering dependence, often without overt pressure. Their care feels natural but quietly shapes your behaviour.
- **Charm Coilers:** Their influence coils around you, one side supportive, the other controlling, making resistance feel futile.

Dealing With The "Drama" Without Any Drama

Managing an 'eight-armer' personality means **freeing yourself from its constraints and recognising the subtle difference between guidance and control.** This means no longer putting others on pedestals or feigning gratitude just for comfort, especially if it clouds your personal judgment.

- Before you share ideas or invest your time, make sure to clearly define roles, set timelines, and outline expected outcomes.
- Be cautious of access to top-tier meetings or elite circles and informal meetings passed off as "casual catchups"; these often lack the necessary structure, as praise and promises are not enough.

- It is essential to meticulously track one's contributions, particularly in shared documents or brainstorming sessions, and to maintain a comprehensive online and offline record of all communications.
- Focus on pulling back and reclaiming your energy. Reclaim your words by saying, *"I decided,"* instead of *"They suggested."*
- Take back your time. Pause before you reply, turn down anything that drains you, and restore your personal rhythm.

Most of all, reclaim your story and tell it on your own terms, unedited by others.

Grey is the New Blue

BLUEGUARD headlined at global panels, but *Anita* knew that *BLUE IS ALL GREY.*

BLUEGUARD stood out in the tech world as a startup mogul, a visionary dealmaker.

Their widespread influence was evident on TEDx stages, at international summits, and in photos alongside unicorn founders and celebrity investors. Their brand and reputation were flawless.

As Anita, a first-time founder launching a climate-tech venture called *REEF OS*, stepped into the BlueGuard Tank, she was greeted by a scent that evoked an ocean of opportunities.

Kai, the CEO, offered a handshake both welcoming and cautionary. *"REEF OS seems a tide we would love to ride. Let's take it across oceans."*

Murphy, the Manager, agreeing with Kai's words, said, *"We are here to cultivate the invested capital." Pearl, an executive,* grinned, saying, *"We will help you grow faster than you think". "You will see. With us, everyone thrives",* said *Coral, another executive,* playfully nudging Anita.

Fundraising, Mentorship calls, design reviews, and investor introductions were the OCTOPUS's subtle tendrils.

In return, she was asked to work from their office for an "integrated approach". Initially, this seemed like the perfect opportunity. With access to advisors, designers, and press, REEF OS grew tenfold, at least on paper.

BLUEGUARD's praise was constant. *"You are part of the family now,"* Murphy said, letting the word 'family' curl around her like a ribbon.

In the blink between now and next, there was a shift.

Her investor calls were rerouted, emails were monitored, and even intern hiring needed approval, and all decisions were now made solely in line with BLUEGUARD's strategy.

When a media feature praised her too highly, BLUEGUARD Team smiled and said, *"Let us keep the spotlight balanced, shall we?"*

Her name faded from press releases; her ideas were reduced to "team contributions." Coral assured her, *"These are just temporary optics."* Yet "temporary" lasted for months. If Anita hesitated, Kai would simply smile and say, *"Trust us, the fire is yours; we are just fanning the spark."*

One night, Anita sat in silence, reflecting on her entrepreneurial path. Even as founder and CEO of a company built from her blood, sweat, and tears, she felt confined.

To reclaim what was hers, she thought of the Blue Whale tactic: deep, strategic, and zen.

Getting a legal team on her side, she re-registered the key intellectual property, obtained board approval under her own name, raised angel investment, and gradually limited access. Each request or attempt at 'alignment' encountered her composed resistance.

Months later, at a press conference, it was announced: *"REEF OS Returns to Founder Leadership."* BLUEGUARD smiled, oblivious. Their OCTOPUS arms now gripped only empty water. Anita sighed, leaving the tank.

She learned to move in a manner where OCTOPUS's arms could not reach. Some creatures hug, some rule and the smartest, just outswim them.

Flippin' The Mirror (Self-Reflection)

One often imagines the OCTOPUS as a formidable entity, manipulatively pulling strings from above. At times, without realising it, we become central figures in others' stories.

Care or guidance can unintentionally turn into control as people start making decisions to meet our expectations. The most subtle forms of power are hardest to spot.

They present themselves as support but gradually crowd out space, creativity, and autonomy. Both in life and work, genuine success stems not from control, but from empowering others to lead themselves. Real leadership is not about being irreplaceable but building spaces where others shine, not disappear in your presence.

Ultimately, we all tend to overextend our influence. Wisdom is knowing when to reach out and when to let go. As *The Alchemist* wisely observes: *"When we strive to become better than we are, everything around us becomes better too."*

YOUR SPACE

The most subtle traps are often disguised as good intent. This is why awareness, rather than accusation, serves as your most reliable guide. It is entirely acceptable to withdraw without engaging in drama. Additionally, it is permissible to safeguard your peace without the necessity of explanation.

Remain close with what feels like breath rather than a burden. In moments of uncertainty, return to yourself.

Use these prompts to spot if an OCTOPUS has ensnared you or if you have been the one ensnaring:

- Which relationships or projects in my life feel comfortable but draining, rather than truly empowering?
- When I give more than I receive, am I choosing this willingly, or have I been subtly steered into this pattern?

- Where have I silently altered my voice, ideas, or boundaries just to maintain harmony?
- In what ways might my guidance, warmth, or support unintentionally foster dependence?
- How do I balance mentorship with control? Am I encouraging growth, or am I shaping others in my own image?

When others hesitate or defer to me, is it because they trust me, or am I unconsciously influencing them?

OCTOPUSES sculpt the world with silent art,
Yet hold its fate within each clever heart.
Do not let yourself become entangled or
controlled like a puppet on strings.

CHAPTER 6

THE HYENA
HAUNTING YOU WITH LAUGHS

The Hyena Wrecks the Orchard

Amy's betrayal haunted *Rachel* with a permanent, silent wound, colder than any missed chance.

People often say that true friendship is like fine wine: the longer it brews, the stronger it becomes, just as Rachel and Amy's friendship did. Both were dreamer-doers, but their temperaments differed greatly.

Amy, like a sprinter, thrived on quick achievements and immediate results.

Rachel, by contrast, was patient and persistent, a marathon runner driven by long-term goals, unconcerned with when, or if, recognition came.

They formed a close bond fuelled by coffee, croissants, late-night study sessions, shared ambitions, and long, thoughtful conversations about the careers they aspired to build post-graduation.

After graduation, Amy joined "*Haus of Hype*," a fast-paced PR startup filled with hustle, paparazzi, and late-night ideas. Soon, she was everywhere - at panels, leadership dinners, and on social media, her posts shining like her diamond ring.

In contrast, Rachel chose the steady path at "*NorthStar Narrative*," enjoying predictable clients, lasting impact, and quiet satisfaction.

At their weekly coffee and croissant meet-ups, Amy often teased Rachel with a playful grin, *"You are settling, Rach. You deserve more than touch base, circle backs, and fixed pay. With your talent, you could already be running your own firm."*

Rachel gave an uncertain smile in response. *"Stability is not a crime, Amy." "Neither is ambition,"* Amy replied with honey-toned and heavy words.

Rachel believed that these statements stemmed from genuine concern.

Eventually, Rachel quit her job to join a budding production house as a creative producer. Although it seemed liberating, the company collapsed within months due to debt and disillusionment.

She called her decision courageous, but in retrospect, it was more like hypnosis crafted by people who appear caring yet seek to control.

The job shimmered for a moment before collapsing. Despite everything, Rachel never blamed Amy, believing some friendships merit forgiveness.

Ironically, Amy's PR startup also collapsed due to staged controversies and internal disputes. While coping with professional setbacks, the two unknowingly drifted apart, a quiet separation born of pride, silence, and bruised egos.

Rachel started freelancing soon after. What began as small projects eventually grew into *"Creative Orchard"*, her own thriving firm. Rachel posted on LinkedIn months later: "*Open to collaborations.*" That same evening, her phone buzzed with a message from Amy. *"Maybe it is time we work together again. Let us bring our old magic back,"* Amy wrote. Rachel also offered to onboard Amy's associates. The message brought nostalgia to both, like old scars often do.

They started working for a client Amy already knew, creating an overly casual atmosphere. Deadlines became vague, and credit was unclear. *"Relax, Rach. Leaders do not let emotions take over,"* Amy said. Rachel stayed quiet, feeling guilty. Maybe I am too controlling, she thought. As the project progressed, Rachel's decisions were increasingly overlooked. Amy started leading calls and rewriting pitches, and as issues arose, she swatted responsibility away and distanced herself from Rachel. Ultimately, the project was shelved.

Rachel mourned not her work but the friendship she thought she had, yet she could do little, since she had insisted on bringing *HYENA* into her *Orchard.*

The Anatomy of a Cackle

HYENA-type personalities hold a captivating presence, appear highly intelligent, and always present themselves as emotionally aware, helpful people.

Beneath this tempting façade, however, hides a predatory mindset.

These individuals subtly exploit the kindness and efforts of others, expertly timing their appearances and emotional responses to manipulate those around them. Instead of breaking bonds or openly confronting anyone, they deceive by feigning support, only to betray trust when least expected.

The Corporate Jungle Where They Thrive

The HYENA thrives as a subtle predator, succeeding through wit, alliances, and careful timing rather than brute strength.

They are found in dynamic or chaotic workplaces because they excel at reading people rather than following processes. Much like their matriarchal clan structure, HYENAS excel at navigating Pack Politics: balancing power dynamics, gossip, and selective loyalty.

With seniors, they are attentive and agreeable; with juniors, they are often dismissive and draining. Their deceptive, fleek attitude and cognitive agility help them mask ambition with an effortless attitude, always calculating beneath the surface. Much like professionals who intervene at the final stage to take credit or influence results, they hunt only when success is assured, opportunistically feeding like survivalists on the kills made by others.

The Spotlight Snatcher

One morning, as *Sid* leaned over her notes, he reassured *Adele*:

"Do not worry, I have got this. You just shine."

She believed him.

Adele launched *Eterna Gems*, a lab-grown diamond startup, in Malaysia. She aimed to shine so brightly that even natural diamonds would feel self-conscious. Every detail mattered, and each investor pitch was a cut closer to perfection.

Recommended by the Board, she recruited Sid, a knowledgeable and accomplished advisor. With his sleek suits and quiet magnetism, he brought Fortune Bouquet for Adele and cupcakes for the team. Admired by all, trusted implicitly, he seemed untouchable.

To the team, he embodied credibility; to Adele, he was the missing glimmer in her vision. Sid addressed Adele as "visionary" in front of venture capitalists but posted on social media, positioning himself as the silent force behind the company.

Adele said, *"Sid, here are the mandatory items for the pitch: market data, growth charts, and projections. I just need your refined report to strengthen the story before we finalise the deck."* Smiling, Sid replied, *"It is your pitch; obviously, it shall shine. No need for refined reports. Just here to highlight your strengths"*. As the clock ticked away, Adele's stress mounted. She ran through her ideas, meticulously double-checking every number, phrase, and slide, except for Sid's "missing" refined report.

Two days before the pitch, a board member with unease in his voice told Adele, *"Sid... when he spoke to the investors, he presented your ideas as if he had shaped your vision and implied that he was the right person to lead and had the entire team's support."*

Adele's chest tightened, a diamond-hard weight. Her head felt hollow.

Sid's every gesture appeared calculated, as though he were performing, and carried a predatory edge.

Sid had stepped into the light she had carved, leaving her shadowed.

The Negrino Nemico

Moving like steam, *Valeria* reshaped herself to fit each room she entered.

In the sun-soaked vineyards of Sicily, the ***Marino family*** had built their artisanal beverage empire called ***Vigna d'Oro*** over three generations. Patiently brewed recipes. Handwritten vendor deals. Sunday board meetings smelled of espresso, oak, and laughter echoing through the courtyard like slow family reunions.

Then came *Valeria.* sleek, worldly, with a Colombian degree, YSL heels, and an exquisite sense of when to speak or simply sip her wine.

Her humble demeanour and helpful smile put everyone at ease. Yet each compliment was carefully calibrated, and every silence was intentional, a setup for something more. She observed which uncle shied away from confrontation, which cousin was anxious with numbers, and who was most receptive to her flattery. Rather than challenging decision-makers, she befriended them, earning their trust as a confidante.

"Zio, should I document the sales report?" she asked, notes in hand. She pushed a file toward Nio and quietly added, *"Your vendor rates needed adjusting, so I fixed them,"* while reassigning key logistics to her old classmate's firm.

Each quiet favour paved the way for her masterstroke. When she finally proposed a new policy that consolidated all external-facing operations under a "Strategic Control Unit to streamline external dealings," the family applauded her dedication. The loophole was that the entire unit would be staffed by her own personnel.

While the signatures dried, Valeria filled a crystal glass with wine. Raising it, she offered a toast: *"To Marinos."* Her voice carried the same subtle complexities as a Bordeaux from their vineyards.

No title change. No blood spilt.
But the reins were hers.

Clean Jungle, Happy Culture

Childhood tales warn us of HYENAS, the friendly sentinel, waiting near hunters for scraps. In the workplace, HYENA personalities exhibit similar behaviours of feeding off confusion and disorder with pure vigilance.

To counter this, teams must protect clarity, credit, and accountability. This would strengthen trust and ensure a workplace where genuine contributions are rewarded, and all members can prosper free from coercive actions.

Pattern Recognition, Not Paranoia

Much like the distorted mirrors at an amusement park, a HYENA's guile warps reality, making deception seem appealing. You perceive teamwork; they see an opportunity. You share laughter until the echo sounds strange.

Here is how to tell if you, too, are caught in the illusion and echo of the *HYENA's Hall of Fame*:

- **Psychological Choreographers:** They position themselves exactly where your sensitivity meets their advantage. In chaotic times, you confide in them, trusting their support. Later, you discover they were quietly cataloguing your weaknesses like case notes, rehearsing lines drawn from your vulnerabilities, and planning their next attack.
- **Meaning Morphers:** HYENAS are amazing alchemists as they refrain from direct theft. They glow with a second-hand radiance, never kindling their own flame.
- **Impeccable Performers:** In their theatre, control is the script, and illusion blends easily with intention. They step into the spotlight just as the scene needs them. When they leave, it is explained before anyone asks why. Their praise for the audience feels rehearsed, encouraging audiences to praise them back.
- **Narrative Hijackers:** They are masterminds in turning a marathon of conversation into a relay, grabbing the baton mid-stride, and running off alone, leaving others questioning or side-tracked.

Dealing With the "Drama" Without Any Drama

- Managing a 'HYENA' personality is not effective with attention or confrontation. These approaches only fuel their disruptive edge.
- Instead, use subtle but assertive responses to acknowledge them, and ensure the conversation remains a collaborative discussion rather than a battle for attention.

HYENAS thrive on ambiguity; create none.

As Don Draper said, "If you do not like what is being said, change the conversation."

Precision and poise set you apart. Let tangible proof and traceability speak for themselves. If they are praised excessively, lightly redirect: *"Yes, we discussed that in the last meeting."*

- HYENAS feed on emotional reactions, so use intentional silence as your resistance.

- Refuse to engage in drama with those who vibe on it; let your consistency win.
- They chase recognition, not real credit.
- Let transparency reveal them, then move on. If escalation is needed, gather allies who have experienced similar situations.

The Cackle Claim

Angela, Senior Designer, had said, *"Impressive idea,"* during his first week. *Aidan* smiled and replied, *"Just a lucky break. I am here to learn from people like you."*

Aidan walked into *AD-dicted*, Berlin's top Ad agency, exuding the presence of a fashion influencer and sporting a smile that could turn criticism into applause. While his portfolio was not groundbreaking, his timing set him apart: He would arrive just moments before the senior partners, Listen enough to reflect the panache of each speaker, and react exactly when needed. He subtly inserted his name into others' ideas, rewording them as his own. In group meetings and discussions, he would boast, *"Our incredible team,"* sugar-coating his words and obscuring credit. Management saw him as a promise coated in finesse, while junior staff regarded him as an elusive ghost that inexplicably showed up in every victory photo.

Angela began to observe Aidan's sly pattern of seeking the spotlight without ever being there for the slog. One noon, she confronted him:

"Aidan, if you're going to reuse my layout, at least credit me."

He glanced up from his laptop and replied, "Angela, creativity is collective. As seniors, we should not make it a personal showpiece?"

A few days later, she learned the client requested "a fresh perspective." Management described her reassignment as an alignment with project needs.

Shortly after, Aidan messaged her: "*These things happen in fast-moving teams. No hard feelings, right?*" The words felt pulled like a pat before a push.

Months later, his name appeared in the company newsletter with the headline, *"Ad-dicted just found its fix—Aidan."* Aidan had become Head of Strategy.

An entire magazine spread was planned to celebrate him, with the interview lined up soon.

Yet, when the journalist asked his coworkers to name his defining campaigns, a heavy silence filled the room; no one could name a single tangible achievement.

Angela paused when it was her turn. The old tremor of doubt returned. She steadied her voice and spoke: *"Aidan has a gift for making others feel seen, yet true leadership is not about being in the spotlight, but about the light that endures after it passes,"*, she said.

The journalist paused, quiet for a moment before thanking her as he left to file his heated report. Angela smiled faintly, aware she had endured his subtle power play without attempting to outshine him.

That line was published, her words shattering the illusion.

By morning, the office echoed with a realisation, a truth: some predators do not bite - they flatter until you forget you are being used.

Aidan read the piece, his jaw clenched, unable to dispute the grace written in black and white. His silence, for the first time, spoke of defeat rather than control.

That evening, he found Angela by the elevator. His voice was low, edged with challenge. *"You really believe a single quote can shift the way people see the world?"* She met his gaze.

"No. But sometimes it forces them to truly see, if only for a moment."

He scoffed, a thin shield for the bruise. *"Ever the optimist."* She arched an eyebrow, unshaken. *"Ever the critic."*

As the elevator doors parted, ironically, the air cackled. In silence.

Flippin' The Mirror (Self-Reflection)

A HYENA persona is not a full identity, but a fleeting instinct that arises when recognition lacks or impostor syndrome sets in. It appears when one exaggerates their role, accepts praise for ideas that are not theirs, or quietly benefits from a peer's setback. These are subtle acts by those weary of being overlooked. The real danger is not what the HYENA persona takes from others, but what it costs within.

The question is not *"Am I a HYENA?"* but *"Have I ever traded authenticity for approval?"*

Notice when appeal replaces honesty or ambition appears as integrity. If fear has ever made you seek the spotlight, pause. The Self-reflection antidote should be a quiet recalibration, an awareness, not a moral judgment.

Your Space

Beneath the HYENA's mystique lies a blueprint for manufacturing momentum and ascending without earning it. They seize the thrones others neglect to defend. You cannot call it treachery if they smiled before, during, and after.

Use these prompts to identify whether a HYENA has attacked you using its canines, or if you were the canine predator:

- Has being praised for your "team spirit" ever felt like your individuality was being quietly erased in barter of someone else's spotlight?
- Have you confused closeness for genuine partnership, assuming you were both building together, when they were standing on your work?
- When others labelled your silence as "grace," was it really peace, or was it the fatigue of always having your truth rewritten by someone else?
- Is rewriting others' insights in your own words an act of collaboration, or does it come from a fear that your originality will not make you stand out?
- Do you adopt outward signs of humility, like gentle smiles or small nods, to intentionally mask your strength because you know that gentleness makes power more palatable?
- If applause ceased today, would your confidence persist, or would silence show that you depend on external validation?

Some predators feed on fear, others on fascination. Turn away before you reflect on the HYENA's illusion.

CHAPTER 7

THE SNAKE
SLITHERING BETWEEN SIDES

Switching Sides in a Heartbeat

And for the first time, the wilderness felt honest - its predators were no longer hidden.

When *Eco Sync AI*, a wildlife-driven tech startup that tracked endangered species through AI-powered microchips, launched in California, it was a wild idea executed wonderfully. *Co-founder Sofia, a zoologist,* brought the soul while *Co-founder Alex, an engineer,* built the system.

They worked in a glass cabin near the ridges of Jackson Hole, coding to the haunting bugles of elk and building momentum.

Jordan was onboarded as a prototype developer.

The founders were convinced, well before signing the contract, with his dialogue, *"I am someone who has found his heartbeat in the project's pulse."* He would map out codes on boards with ease, and the entire team channelised those into strategies.

Everything was on track until the invitation to attend the "*Gaia-Next Summit*" dropped in.

At that event, he encountered Wild Vanta, their rival firm.

Amid the wine glasses clinking and caviar being sampled, Wild Vanta's CEO, impressed by his prototype demonstration, discreetly offered Jordan equity and a sleeker board title, saying, *"You are far too talented to play second fiddle, Jordan. With us, you would be leading the jogging track."*

Although Jordan initially brushed it aside with a fake laugh and sarcastic reply, "*sure*", he could not quite dismiss the proposition.

The first shift was almost imperceptible, zoning in and out, when the founders were in the limelight.

Then came the guarded screens and secretive messages exchanged under dim lights.

"Just share a sample of the code. We will provide feedback, maybe collaborate later," said the rival company. Jordan hesitated but then rationalised that sharing might help EcoSync AI grow in a new direction.

One file led to another as the rival's curiosity intensified.

Eventually, they presented him with a private contract, promising a team, substantial funding, and well-earned recognition.

Soon, he was covertly rewriting EcoSync AI's algorithms, weaving in encrypted lines that replicated its core logic - a secret clone synchronised with the rival's servers. Watching the lines fall into place, he grinned at his screen.

The serpent was already coiling, waiting for the perfect moment to strike.

Reaching the half-year mark, Wild-Vanta outpaced the market with a prototype like Eco Sync AI's new work, which was supposed to be their breakthrough neural tag.

By the time Alex noticed irregular code behaviour, the system had crashed.

EcoSync AI's prototype, once breathing with promise, lay hollow.

Only one person had access to the final launch project. Only one person said all the right things before disappearing with a handwritten resignation, no forwarding address, and a LinkedIn post that read: ***"Evolution requires leaving skins behind."*** Sofia's face paled. Alex fumed.

When confronted, Jordan looked almost relieved.

He replied, saying, *"I just explored an opportunity. I did not betray my pulse."*

The wilderness outside echoed with silence. Jordan shed the *"purpose"* and *"pulse"* like a snake's skin. Seamlessly. Shamelessly.

The Anatomy of a Hiss

There is a reason the phrase "*SNAKE in the grass*" has endured for centuries: it points to a danger that lies not in overt attacks, but in stealth.

- People with snake-like personalities are rarely aggressive or openly disruptive.
- Instead, they operate with quiet calculation, adapting to every change not to grow, but to evade responsibility.

They dodge confrontation; instead, they reposition themselves to align with the winning side. Their loyalty is a temporary garment, shed and replaced as circumstances change. Realising they were never truly by your side hurts more than their eventual departure.

The Corporate Jungle Where They Thrive

A serpent is more subtle than any beast of the field. In the work matrix, the most intuitive and vigilant characters restructure our inward and outward systems.

- These SNAKE-type personalities will not chase attention but study the soul and its environment on a deeper level and slither you in silence.
- You will not guess the 5 Ws (*Who, Where, When, What & Why*) and 1 H (*How*), but only see the aftermath of the mess they leave.

We have all met them: the colleague who played both sides until everything fell apart, the relative who turned legacy into leverage, the intermediaries who revealed just enough truth to stay useful but never truly loyal. They wind themselves around you, leaving you suffocated before you can comprehend that it is too late to escape.

The Coiled Promotion

Cratos Company, a high-tech construction machinery firm with global branches, truly lived up to its name: God of Strength. Its machines were formidable, and its employees a carefully cultivated force.

In Delhi, *Vishwa* exemplified both. Swift, precise, and internationally recognised, he managed multiple departments while leading the Sales team.

During pitches, he occasionally disclosed sensitive information to secure clients.

This behaviour was overlooked until a US resource provider flagged data irregularities.

Monitors flickered red; fingers paused on keyboards. Anxiety drowned out the machines.

Colleagues scrambled as emails pinged like gunfire, amplifying every error. Whispers darted from cubicle to cubicle: *"Was it her?" "Check his logs." Anya* whispered in panic, *"The reports refuse to match."*

Vishwa, calm and unflustered, said, *"Step back. Observe first. Solutions follow."*

Moving with quiet intent, Vishwa rested a hand on Anya's shoulder, whispered to Abhi, and made an offhand remark pointing out a minor oversight by another team - neither accusing nor obvious. With each gentle manoeuvre, he deflected attention from himself.

By evening, Anya and Abhi were suspended on grounds of 'suspicion'.

Anya's voice shook. *"I thought you were..." Abhi completed her sentence, "helping us". "I am here to help you always. We are all together in this Witch-Jungle Hunt. I am so sorry you have to survive through this sudden attack,"* Vishwa reassured.

When the US client and resource provider conference was announced, ironically, Vishwa was chosen to lead the *"Compliance of Ethics"* as his impeccable record, thoroughly documented and flagged for risk, remained unquestioned.

He maintained his *"Wheedler"* ascent through relentless loyalty and subdued manipulation. Anya, Abhi, and the other staff all felt a little heartbroken by the creeping character and his created confusion.

Once, they believed him to be a king, and in a way, he was. But a ***Cobra King***!

The Plastered Support

As *Ross* exited, clutching the new grant, the museum lights flickered - cold, clinical, and slippery as snakes.

Ross and *Emily*, once rival classmates, now established scientists, worked together at the *Code of the Wild Museum*, decoding extinct species' DNA for ecological restoration. Lab benches, pipettes, and a quiet truce were now shared between them.

When Emily's research paper got selected for full funding and an experimental grant, she cried tears of happiness. *"WE did it, our efforts won,"* she told Ross. He smiled. *"YOU deserve it, Em."*

Days later, whispers crept along the marble corridors. Some quipped that *Bridgerton* had come alive in the museum, with *Lady Whistledown* herself publishing the latest gossip. Her data was called "too good to be true," her mentor's visits "too frequent", and her success "too sudden and convenient".

Ross noticed Emily gazing at the memo. *"Hey, Em, don't lose yourself,"* he said gently. *"I hope your next proposal will outshine all of ours, like always."* He offered comfort with a gentle touch on her shoulder, his eyes reflecting the light like glass.

At The Code of the Wild, evolution became deception. Now, the Fork-tongued ruled the Wild.

Clean Jungle, Happy Culture

Imagine a serpent slipping into spaces governed by unspoken rules and ambiguous processes, twisting narratives, and undermining morals and trust. Seems devastating, right?

In the realm of ambition and influence, a wise adage states, *"You cannot make a Tomelette without breaking some Gregs."*

This line from *Succession* serves as a profound lesson about culture, illustrating how unchecked ambition can masquerade as eloquence, leading to the downfall of systems when manipulation is mistaken for competence. By fostering a mindset that prioritises fortifying the environment over fearing a serpent's lunge, trust is gradually built and sustained among peers over the long term. If damage has occurred, let it serve as your audit trail: dissect the breach and track what was tolerated. Learn from silence, avoiding cynicism while striving for precision. This ensures a deliberate approach to maintaining a healthy and harmonious work life, while avoiding toxic 'SNAKE-type' individuals.

Pattern Recognition, Not Paranoia

Playing the corporate game of Snakes & Ladders, every dice roll determines who climbs the ladder and who gets swallowed by the snakes.

You may not always be able to avoid the snakes, but by recognising these patterns in advance, you can protect yourself before they bring you down:

- **The Silent Tactician:** They avoid confrontation, always calculating. Each conversation is a subtle setup, and every compliment, a coil tightening in anticipation of future gain.
- **The Diplomat Without Depth:** Their composure is merely a mask for caution. When they appear neutral, it is not out of any desire for peace, but rather a strategy to position themselves nearer to power.

- **The Intuitive Opportunist:** They detect weakness more quickly than most perceive danger. To the ambitious, they present themselves as allies; to the insecure, as mentors until they are no longer needed.
- **The Two-Faced Advisor:** They function in duality: at one moment, they echo your vision; the next, they mirror your competitor's strategy, guaranteeing they benefit no matter who comes out on top.
- **The Emotional Minimalist:** Like snakes conserving venom, they hold onto warmth, releasing it only when it serves a purpose. They offer little and take much. The Narrative Molter:
- **They rarely invent stories;** instead, they shed and reshape them. By the time you notice a hint, the story has already been rewritten in their favour.

Dealing With The "Drama" Without Any Drama

To handle SNAKE individuals effectively, you must anticipate their actions and stay ahead, rather than reacting hastily, emotionally, or trailing behind.

- Do not confuse charm with substance or diplomacy with reliability.
- Watch how people act around powerful individuals and whether they seek those who can benefit them. Loyalty is not guaranteed by the absence of disloyalty; focus on consistency over flattery.
- Share less to keep control. Some people seek information to use against you.
- Build a supportive, trustworthy network based on facts, not gossip. Spend time with people who value authenticity over rumours.

Maintain a clear, factual space to neutralise their tactics. Rather than responding with aggression or dramatic confrontations, rely on structure and self-regulation. If you must confront, do so calmly and confidently to avoid confusion. Sometimes, silence is most effective, as it cannot be misrepresented.

The Poisoned Tea

Kisho, twenty-one and full of youthful energy, lingered like a shadow - attentive, grateful, and loyal beside *Akira*, a trailblazing Japanese entrepreneur. Though bound to Akira by obligation rather than blood, Kisho was entrusted to his care after a deathbed promise made by Kisho's parents.

Without hesitation, Akira honoured this vow, welcoming Kisho and his brothers into the fold of her family and business, Midorie Trading Co., nestled in the peaceful lanes of Kyoto. Akira taught them about the tea trade, trust, and everything in between.

One evening, a minor miscount caught Akira's attention. *"Kisho-chan, this batch is off by two boxes. Please be diligent next time, and always."*

Kisho nodded awkwardly, yet inside, his pride smouldered - too strong and too fragile to admit fault.

At a family gathering weeks later, Kisho reunited with his cousin Haruto. As they chatted over sake, Haruto mentioned the worldwide surge in matcha's popularity. Kisho's "caffeine" kicked in. He remembered Midorie's dormant resources and untapped warehouse space.

A plan quickly formed: collaborate with Haruto, invest Midorie's assets, and create *"Matcha Mafia"* with the company's support.

To make matters worse, Kyoto was flooded, inventory destroyed, and panic swept through Midorie. Akira called an emergency meeting. *"We need a plan of action. I want everyone's input,"* she said, concerned. In the midst of chaos, Kisho remained calm, leaning back with steady eyes as Akira's gaze found him.

"Kisho... the asset transfer documents?"

He proudly claimed,

"Oh, those? I adjusted them for growth. Invested the assets into a Matcha production venture with Haruto, under the name 'Matcha Mafia'".

A pin-drop silence settled over the room, as if everyone were stunned by tea suddenly spilling from the vessel. Akira blinked, shock and awe swelling in her chest. The boy she had raised now rewrote loyalty in the shadows, managing to do right and wrong at the same time.

His actions were exactly right enough to be profitable, but wrong enough to destroy her trust.

It felt like the sting of a Snake. *"I never lost sight of the endgame,"* Kisho replied, smiling faintly, free of guilt or hesitation.

But snakes forget that even venom has its antidote.

She reviewed Matcha Mafia's documents and discovered a loophole regarding the shares.

Quietly, Akira activated the safety net she had built over the years - a silent chain of loyal investors and dormant clauses. Akira was not a dramatic avenger. There was neither confrontation nor outrage - only strategy, experience, and equanimity.

Through her network, she acquired controlling shares of Matcha Mafia before Kisho could even celebrate his supposed triumph.

When the news broke, Kisho was flabbergasted and stormed into Akira's cabin. Before he could say a word, Akira said, *"In business, the calmest cup hides the fiercest brew. You named it Matcha Mafia - fitting, because now, I run it,"* as she whisked herself a cup of matcha.

The snake had struck first, but the queen owned the garden.

Flippin' The Mirror (Self-Reflection)

A snake moves on from its shed skin, but we must reflect on our past. The real challenge with some people is realising how long we have put up with them, often due to misplaced hope in their potential. Some SNAKES seem kind, echoing our values and lowering our guard. Our reflection must remain honest and constructive. Not every deceiver means harm, but ignoring our instincts has a price. Forgiving is not forgetting; rebuilding trust requires clear boundaries. If you have changed yourself to suit draining people, notice which parts you considered negotiable; that is where healing begins. Wisdom means integrating experience without losing yourself. In a world of snakes, stay grounded and astute because not every smooth connection is safe.

Your Space

You may not always be able to eliminate the snakes from your life, but you can certainly diminish their influence.

By sharpening your awareness, you enhance your vision; setting boundaries helps to preserve your peace, and trusting yourself makes you resilient.

There is no need to retaliate; just stop handing over the knife.

- When did someone's confidence feel more like a performance than presence, and how long did it take for you to see through it?
- Have you ever confused someone's outward composure with their actual character? If so, what did you learn about trust from that experience?
- If betrayal were a sound, which moment in your life still reverberates with it, and what inner strength did you find in the silence that followed?
- Do you seek control because you crave it, or because it is the only way you have ever learned to communicate?
- Which part of you believes that winning justifies shedding every layer, even if one of them is your own truth?
- When loyalty and ambition conflict, which voice prevails within you, and why do you obey it?

A snake may die at dusk, yet its cunning wakes at dawn;
Keep eyes wide, act soft, lest its fangs catch you withdrawn.

EPILOGUE
THE RISE AFTER THE FALL

There comes a moment when you stop asking, *"Why me?"* and start whispering, *"Thank you."* Not because the pain was fair, but because it was formative.

What started as a quest for revenge, meant to prove, expose, and demand, gradually transformed into light. It was not a *blinding light,* but one that gently *guides you home,* the way a song finds its way through the darkness.

The light exposed everything I had avoided: my own patterns, choices, and blind spots. Each person, even those who broke me, served as a parallel reflection, revealing what I needed to heal and let go of, and leading me towards who I was meant to become and be.

Once I stopped blaming the world for what I attracted and started owning what I allowed, that silent reckoning changed everything.

This story is no longer about them. It is about reclaiming my peace, my power, my pulse. I know the tunnel is long and dark, but I have seen the light at its end. And now, I choose to chase that light itself.

A true rise after the fall: AN EVOLUTION!

CONCLUSION
WHEN YOU CAN NAME THEM, YOU CAN STEP AWAY

If you have reached this point in the book, it is likely that one or more of these personalities felt uncomfortably familiar. Perhaps a face appeared in your mind. Perhaps a conversation replayed itself. Perhaps a long-standing confusion suddenly made sense.

That is not accidental.

The people who slowly damage careers, businesses, and confidence rarely arrive as obvious threats. They do not announce themselves as manipulators, blockers, or exploiters. They arrive as dependable colleagues, caring seniors, generous patrons, supportive friends, or inspiring storytellers. They blend into our everyday lives so seamlessly that by the time we feel the impact, we are already entangled.

This book was not written to label people as villains. It was written to help you recognise patterns. Because patterns, when unnamed, quietly take control.

Once you can name the pattern, the confusion lifts. You stop asking why progress always stalls in certain relationships. You stop blaming yourself for feeling drained or guilty. You stop explaining away behaviour that repeatedly harms you.

Clarity does not create conflict. It creates distance where distance is needed, and discernment where blind trust once lived.

A Personal Exit Plan: How People Quietly Reclaim Their Power

Leaving a damaging dynamic does not always mean walking away dramatically. In most real-life situations, it happens in quieter, more strategic ways.

The first step is identification.

Somewhere in this book, you recognised the animal you are dealing with most closely. It could be in your workplace, your business partnership, your family, or even within yourself. Once that recognition happens, denial loses its grip.

The second step is understanding how the pattern is sustained.

Every personality described in this book survives because something feeds it — access, attention, trust, credit, patience, or silence. When those inputs remain unchanged, the behaviour continues unquestioned. When they are reduced, the dynamic shifts.

You do not need to change your nature to protect yourself. You only need to change what access you give.

You may stop oversharing with the Snake, stop waiting endlessly on the Termite, stop justifying yourself to the Donkey, stop seeking approval from the Fly, stop accepting "help" that comes with control from the Octopus, stop giving credit to the Hyena, or stop offering your story to the Cuckoo.

What changes is not your attitude, but your availability.

As access reduces, you will notice something important. The drama lessens. The guilt fades. The pressure eases. In some cases, resistance appears — not because you are wrong, but because the pattern is losing its grip.

And then, almost quietly, something returns.

- Your clarity
- Your pace
- Your confidence

This book does not promise that you will never encounter these personalities again. They exist everywhere. What it gives you is something far more valuable, the ability to recognise them early, respond wisely, and protect what matters most.

Once you can name the animal, you no longer live inside the cage.

And that, in the end, is the real freedom.